Christopher Fry

Twayne's English Authors Series

Kinley E. Roby, Editor
Northeastern University

TEAS 479

Christopher Fry
Photograph by Caroline Hughes

Christopher Fry

By Glenda Leeming

Twayne Publishers
A Division of G. K. Hall & Co. • *Boston*

Christopher Fry
Glenda Leeming

Copyright 1990 by G. K. Hall & Co.
All rights reserved.
Published by Twayne Publishers
A division of G. K. Hall & Co.
70 Lincoln Street
Boston, Massachusetts 02111

Copyediting supervised by Barbara Sutton.
Book production by Gabrielle B. McDonald.
Typeset in 11 pt. Garamond
by Compositors Corporation, Cedar Rapids, Iowa.

First published 1990.
10 9 8 7 6 5 4 3 2 1

The paper used in this publication meets the minimum requirements
of American National Standard for Information Sciences—Permanence
of Paper for Printed Library Materials, ANSI Z39.48–1984. ∞™

Printed and bound in the United States of America.

Library of Congress Cataloging-in-Publication Data

Leeming, Glenda.
    Christopher Fry / by Glenda Leeming.
        p.   cm. — (Twayne's English authors series ; TEAS 479)
    Includes bibliographical references.
    ISBN 0-8057-6998-6 (alk. paper)
    1. Fry, Christopher—Criticism and interpretation.   I. Title.
II. Series.
PR6011.R9Z74   1990
822'.914—dc20   90-4395
                                                        CIP

Contents

About the Author

A freelance writer and critic, Glenda Leeming received her undergraduate and graduate degrees from University College London and is the author of, among other books, *Wesker the Playwright* (1983) and *Poetic Drama* (1989).

Preface

> Sometimes when I am trying to work I think of the picture of myself which emerges from the press-cuttings, and it seems, in a way, very splendid. I see a man reeling intoxicated with words; they flow in a golden—or perhaps pinchbeck—stream from his mouth: they start out at his ears; they burst like rockets and jumping crackers and catherine-wheels round his head; they spring in wanton sport at his feet and trip him; but trip him or not he loves them. . . . Then, having looked at this picture and marvelled, I turn back to my typewriter. Like an ancient Red Indian chief, I sit for some hours in silence. At last I am ready to speak, and say "How," or perhaps some slightly longer word. My two fingers withdraw from the typewriter and the night wears dumbly on towards the dawn.[1]

Thus Christopher Fry placed the critical image of himself as playwright (at this stage [1952] known as author of *A Phoenix Too Frequent, The Lady's Not for Burning,* and *Venus Observed*) beside his own picture of himself as painstaking craftsman, images that contrast equally with the Fry of academic studies, which tend to concentrate heavily on the religious significance of his plays. A fourth alternative view might be that of audiences, elusive now but occasionally hinted at in reviews or deducible from box office figures. Ideally I would have liked to reconcile these images and to set the ideas evident in the plays against their potential realization in the text and the actual realization in a series of productions, but the imperfect and contradictory accounts of reviews and reminiscences of the first—and later—productions make this difficult. Of course, one can state more or less firmly that the text is, for instance, unclear at a certain stage of the action, but one can never foresee whether the inspiration of a director may reveal the hitherto unsuccessful idea as triumphantly effective. T. S. Eliot, with his own experiments in this same area of poetic drama, concluded prematurely that the many attempts to present the Eumenides in *The Family Reunion* proved that they were unstageable, only to have a stunning *coup de théâtre* justify his Furies in Michael Elliot's productions in the sixties.[2]

Critics of the forties and fifties in London had their own views of the rules to which a play should conform, and amid reviews that commented on the audience's interest and amusement while complaining about lack of plot, there emerges an idea of the sort of qualities demanded—for instance "tension" and "smoothness." These are among the virtues of the well-made play: the smooth and logical development of the strong plot with tension, or suspense, kept dependent on the withheld solution of a mystery or problem. The fact that these qualities were being sought suggests that critics and perhaps the happier audiences did not perceive what other elements they were being offered—that is, the ideas. The clarity, or rather recognizability, of Fry's ideas becomes a theatrical problem because it is not enough to decode the themes and symbols in the text; one needs also to try to judge whether the text expresses these ideas adequately for them to be presented and grasped at the speed of dramatic presentation. Fry said that there was no great obstacle in the fact that he was a Christian writing for an audience perhaps of nonbelievers: "We are all involved in a process which it is simpler to call God than anything else, and if I can manage to write about—not theories—but what it feels like to be a living man, in fact, I am writing about what every man feels, even if in doubt or rejection."[3] That is, the audience will recognize the truths Fry is expressing; though perhaps in terms other than the religious formulation that Fry would use.

Tentatively, then, one can say that a successful production, in whatever style, should convey the author's ideas forcibly enough to be recognized, if in secular terms, by the audience. I have tried to show what basis the text gives for such productions, as well as describing the other qualities that have caused Fry's great popularity with audiences and readers.

There is no collected edition of Christopher Fry's works. I have used the convenient three-volume Oxford University Press edition, which contains all of Fry's plays up to *Curtmantle*. Although the volumes are not named or numbered, my citations in this book refer to them as volume 1 (*The Boy with a Cart, The Firstborn, Venus Observed*), volume 2 (*A Phoenix Too Frequent, Thor, with Angels, The Lady's Not for Burning*), and volume 3 (*A Sleep of Prisoners, The Dark is Light Enough, Curtmantle*). This is not the order of publication; it is based on the early origins of the plays in the 1970 volume (my volume 1). *A Yard of Sun* is available only in the individual edition of 1970, and *One Thing More* is published by King's College London (1986). Because lines are not numbered in any of these texts and some of the plays have no act or scene divisions, reference is to page numbers.

My most grateful acknowledgment is to Christopher Fry for his patience and tolerance, as well as his helpful explanations of his plays, his intentions, and their realization; any quotations from Fry not otherwise attributed are from personal conversations with him. Without these conversations, this book would have been less full and less informative; any inaccuracies and obscurities are, of course, my own.

I would also like to thank Oxford University Press for permission to quote from Fry's plays.

Glenda Leeming

Chronology

1907   Christopher Fry born 18 December, the younger son of Charles John Harris and Emma Marguerite, née Hammond, in Bristol, England.

1913   Mother moves with her two sons and her elder sister to Bedford. In September Fry begins school at the Froebel Kindergarten attached to the Froebel Training College, Bedford.

1918   Enters Bedford Modern School as day boy. World War I ends.

1922–1926   Writes various juvenilia, including the plays *Armageddon* and *Youth and the Peregrines*.

1926   Leaves school. Teaches temporarily at the school attached to the Froebel Training College.

1927   Spends short time as a general assistant at a small theater company in Bath, doing acting and secretarial work.

1928   Teaches in a preparatory school.

1929   Holds various theatrical jobs.

1934   Works as director of the semiprofessional Tunbridge Wells Repertory Players. Directs British premier of George Bernard Shaw's *A Village Wooing* in a double bill with his own *Youth and the Peregrines*.

1935   Writes *Open Door* (commissioned by Dr. Barnardo's Homes, a national charity organization that operates homes for destitute children, and based on the life of Thomas John Barnardo, the organization's founder), which tours for two years. Writes musical comedy *She Shall Have Music*, produced at Saville Theatre.

1936   Marries Phyllis Hart.

1938   Writes *The Boy with a Cart* for performance for the local church in Coleman's Hatch, Sussex.

1939   *The Boy with a Cart* performed in the bishop's garden, Chichester. Begins writing *The Firstborn* but sets it aside to complete *The Tower* for the Tewkesbury Festival. *The Open*

Door, a pageant play, written for the Girls' Friendly Society and performed at the Albert Hall. The Frys move to Oxfordshire, and Fry becomes director of the Oxford Playhouse.

1940 Drafted; enters army in a noncombatant company.

1944 Ill in military hospital. Discharged from army. Returns to Oxford Playhouse.

1946 *A Phoenix Too Frequent* produced at the Mercury Theatre in May; revived at Arts Theatre in November.

1948 *The Lady's Not for Burning* performed at the Arts Theatre. *Thor, with Angels* commissioned and performed at Canterbury Festival. *The Firstborn* performed at the Edinburgh Festival.

1949 *The Lady's Not for Burning* revived at the Globe Theatre with John Gielgud.

1950 *Venus Observed* performed at the St. James's Theatre, with Laurence Olivier. Translates Jean Anouilh's *L'Invitation au château* as *Ring around the Moon. The Boy with a Cart* produced professionally at the Lyric Theatre, Hammersmith, with Richard Burton.

1951 Writes *A Sleep of Prisoners* for the Festival of Britain celebrations; performed in churches on tour, including in Oxford and London.

1953 Writes commentary for coronation film, *A Queen Is Crowned,* and script for film of *The Beggars Opera.*

1954 *The Dark Is Light Enough* performed at the Aldwych Theatre, with Edith Evans.

1955 Translates Jean Anouilh's *The Lark* and Jean Giraudoux's *La Guerre de Troie n'aura pas lieu* as *Tiger at the Gates.*

1958 Translates Giraudoux's *Pour Lucrèce* as *Duel of Angels.* Writes screenplay for *Ben Hur.*

1961 World premiere of *Curtmantle* in Tilburg, Holland.

1962 *Curtmantle* performed at Edinburgh Festival; transferred to Aldwych Theatre in October. Translates Giraudoux's *Judith.* Writes screenplay for *Barabbas.*

1965 Writes children's book, *The Boat That Mooed.*

1966 Writes screenplay for *The Bible: In the Beginning.*

1968 Television adaptation of Anne Brontë's *The Tenant of Wildfell Hall.*

1970 *A Yard of Sun* performed at the Nottingham Playhouse. Translates Henrik Ibsen's *Peer Gynt.*

1973 Television series of four plays: *The Brontës of Haworth.*

1975 Translates Edmond Rostand's *Cyrano de Bergerac.*

1977 Writes television play, *Sister Dora.*

1978 Writes *Can You Find Me,* a "family history."

1986 Writes *One Thing More,* commissioned jointly by Chelmsford Cathedral and BBC; performed in November in Chelmsford Cathedral, broadcast later in the same month.

Chapter One
Fry: His Life and Career

Christopher Fry is best known to the average theatergoer or reader for his West End successes—*A Phoenix Too Frequent, The Lady's Not for Burning, Venus Observed,* and *The Dark Is Light Enough.* When these were first produced, audiences responded immediately to the verbal wit and the sensual evocation of his imagery—that is, the appeal of his language—rather than to the fact that they knew the plays were written in verse or conveyed certain values. Fry, more than most other playwrights of his time, primarily appealed to—and surprised—the audience's linguistic expectations.

Fewer of the general public are aware of Fry's religious plays, yet they form an important part of his work, nourished as it was by three historic movements or tendencies: the religious drama movement, the poetic drama movement, and the postwar hunger for lightness and expansiveness. The last, and most temporary factor, of the three points to another of Fry's characteristics: the ultimately positive philosophy that the plays offer, though there are many qualifications and some pessimism within their message. Arnold Hinchcliffe calls Fry "as religious a dramatist as Eliot,"[1] and even the conflict and stress of *The Firstborn* and, to some extent, *A Sleep of Prisoners* is reconciled at the level of an overruling divine plan. The comedies not only present that plan through witty and amusing dialogue but explicitly confirm that the mundane world is pleasant and beautiful. Critics persistently linked Fry's name with that of T. S. Eliot as joint leaders of the revival of poetic drama in the forties and fifties, but Eliot's religious philosophy was less cheerful, and even *The Cocktail Party,* with its highly comic and ironic dialogue, suggests that this world is to be endured rather than enjoyed.

Fry's background includes more religious influences than poetic or dramatic ones. The name Fry that he adopted is that of his maternal grandmother; he says, "I was brought up believing the Frys were Quakers . . . but the evidence is so slight."[2] Born in 1907, he has few memories of his father, Charles Harris, formerly a builder who in 1904 decided to become a poorly paid lay preacher but died in 1911 when Fry, his younger son, was only three. His widowed mother was left to bring up two little boys alone, on a tiny legacy from her own mother and some contributions from her in-laws. In

1913 she pooled her resources with an elder sister and went to live in Bedford. A major attraction of the town was its good educational opportunities. Christopher went first to the experimental Froebelian school, attached to the Froebel College for training teachers, which made a special point of encouraging creativity in pupils, and then followed his brother to the distinguished independent Bedford Modern School.

Fry had no father or brother old enough to be called up in World War I, but some of his cousins and friends were killed, and some soldiers who were billeted in his house were also later killed. The house was on the road to the cemetery, where those who had returned home to die were buried: "These slow processions up Gladstone Street happened so often that even now when I hear the pounding notes of the funeral march, the thuds of the opening bars followed by that aching effort to lift the notes higher, I also hear the rattle of the gun-carriage and the irregular clatter of the reined-in horses" (*Can You Find Me*, 243). By the end of the war, peace was something that the child Christopher could hardly remember, and it is not surprising that soldiers, or warriors, and ex-soldiers appear in all but two of his plays, bringing up repeatedly the issues of violence and sudden death that had been part of boyhood for his generation.

Fry showed interest and talent in several fields from childhood onward but did not settle firmly on any one. He had taught himself to play the piano by ear at an early age and composed tunes that he played at school, he wrote plays for the other children, and he distinguished himself in a competitive art examination. He took Greek lessons with the idea of entering the ministry, but when he left school in 1926 at eighteen, he spent some time teaching at the Froebelian school while he considered what he wanted to do.

It is important that Fry's career for the next fifteen years lay mainly in the theater, including various fringe activities such as cabaret, because this gave him a considerable professional experience that other poetic dramatists of the period lacked. After leaving the Froebelian school, he spent six months in Bath doing acting and secretarial work at the Citizen House Theatre, and then he fell back on teaching again for two years. During the late 1920s and early 1930s, Fry moved from job to job in repertory and other theatrical ventures. All this time he was hoping to write, and it was in 1932 that he spent the memorable summer with poet and biographer Robert Gittings that he described in the dedication to *A Sleep of Prisoners* as a "holiday from my full time failure to make a living":

I had written almost nothing for five or six years, and I was to write almost nothing again for five years following, but the two months we spent at Thorn, two months (it seems to me now) of continuous blazing sunshine, increased in me the hope that one day the words would come. It was all very well that I should look obstinately forward to plays which I showed no sign of writing. It was an extraordinary faith which made you also look obstinately forward to them. The ten years in which you loyally thought of me as a writer when clearly I wasn't, your lectures to me on my self-defensive mockery of artists, and those two leisure months under the Quantocks, were things of friendship which kept me in a proper mind.[3]

Two years later, working with the semiamateur Tunbridge Wells Repertory company, Fry put on one of his own plays, *Youth and the Peregrines*, in a double bill with George Bernard Shaw's *A Village Wooing* (a British premier for the latter, granted by Shaw with typical generosity to the unknown young director), but this had been written in 1924, and perhaps the "almost nothing" of this period is represented by *She Shall Have Music*, a musical comedy that had a short run at the Saville Theatre in 1935 and for which Fry had written the music as well as the lyrics. In 1936 he married Phyllis Hart, whom he met at Tunbridge Wells; she was English but had taken her degree at a Canadian university.

After leaving the repertory, the Frys lived in poverty, but Christopher was at last writing plays that were produced: *Open Door*, which had been commissioned by Dr. Barnardo's Homes to commemorate the life of their founder, toured the country for two years, and *Thursday's Child* was performed by amateurs in the Albert Hall in 1938. Most import t was the writing of *The Boy with a Cart* in 1938 for a church festival in the Sussex village where the Frys were living. This festival, though local, was attended by various influential people and put Fry in touch with the religious drama movement and directly or indirectly led to further commissions, such as *The Tower*, performed in 1939 at Tewkesbury Festival, and eventually to his West End successes.

Fry's writing for the Oxford Playhouse led to his replacing Leslie French as its artistic director when the latter went off to make a film, but the war soon caught up with Fry. Although he was a pacifist, opposed to taking life, he was not prepared to refuse all involvement in the war. Like many others, he found this a painful dilemma; even imperfect knowledge of the atrocities of Hitler's Germany showed a victory for the Nazis would mean destruction of all the human values he prized: "It would have been simply a martyrdom. And I didn't feel sure that martyrdom was right." So he was drafted into a noncombatant corps in the army. He served with, among others, the biographer George Painter; his own critic and biographer, Derek Stanford; and actor Michael Gough. Fry was ill with pneumonia during the war, and though he pored over the half-finished *The Firstborn*, he was unable to do more than rewrite and rearrange. The stress and deprivation of this period led to a breakdown, and Fry was discharged in 1944. Gittings suggests that "the somewhat horrific experiences of a Military Hospital to some extent contributed to [the character] of Thomas Mendip," though Fry himself does not think so.[4]

Just before the war, Fry had moved to a small rented cottage in Oxfordshire with his wife and young son; here he returned and was doing further work for the Oxford Playhouse when his friend from the festival drama period of the late 1930s, E. Martin Browne, invited him to contribute to a season of poetic drama in a small fringe theater in London. The result was *A Phoenix Too Frequent* (1946), marking the culmination and end of Fry's apprentice work. For the next fifteen years or so, Fry was one of the most popular and successful dramatists in Great Britain. Although his next plays on religious subjects, the finally completed *The Firstborn* and *Thor, with Angels,* both produced in 1948, were not enthusiastically received, *The Lady's Not for Burning* (1948) was a comedy, appropriately subtitled "A Spring Comedy," that became a classic in the repertoire. His other comedies, *Venus Observed* (1950) and *The Dark Is Light Enough* (1954) followed, labeled, respectively, autumn and winter comedies, as well as the remarkable though lesser known *A Sleep of Prisoners,* commissioned for the Festival of Britain in 1951.

Fry was in much demand for work in the media. He translated several plays by the French writers Anouilh and Giraudoux and later in the fifties worked on film scripts in Italy. The Frys had a house in London, as well as one in the country, but avoided much participation in theatrical socializing: several friends and acquaintances have commented on Christopher Fry's retiring nature, and Phyl Fry was equally retiring. By the late fifties, however, the British theater was absorbing new dramatic fashions. Fry's plays did not fit with either the revival of naturalism or with the contrary trend of absurdist drama from Europe. Fry recalled, "For a time I went through a kind of crisis of confidence in my own ability to express the world as I saw it in terms of the modern theater," and he was grateful to T. S. Eliot for giving encouragement and support at this period ("Talking of Henry," 186). His first play to deal with authentic historical characters and events, *Curtmantle* (1962), in a production by the Royal Shakespeare Company, was only moderately successful; some critics liked it very much, but others thought it too long and shapeless. At this point Fry's plays went into eclipse, except in the amateur and provincial theater, where the comedies continued to be produced.

Fry left the stage for ten years, returning with the little-known *A Yard of Sun* in 1970, which completed the seasons as "A Summer Comedy" and ousted the tentative claim of *A Phoenix Too Frequent* to fill that niche. Sixteen years later, at seventy-nine, Fry accepted the commission to write another festival play, *One Thing More,* on the story of Caedmon. By this time, the attitude of critics had changed. *Lady* was televised at Christmas 1987 at the time of Fry's eightieth birthday, and several journals published celebratory tributes to the writer, no longer castigating the plays for not being Beckettian or Pinteresque but accepting them as brilliant verbally comic products of their time.

Chapter Two
Religious and Poetic Drama and *The Boy with a Cart*

All Fry's early writing was theatrical in one way or another—comedy, pageant, musical—and he was never drawn to write novels. His religious interests and the chance of certain opportunities and friendships channeled his writing away from revue and the well-made play into a genre that gave scope to his particular linguistic gifts.

The Religious Drama Movement

Religious drama continues as a genre. As long as plays with a religious theme are performed in churches or specifically for church festivals, the form can be said to survive. Fry's most recent play was written for and performed in Chelmsford Cathedral in 1986. But the religious drama movement that developed in England in the first half of the twentieth century was much more organized and flourishing. Some of the dramatic products could be classified as popular theater; some was wholly amateur and some wholly professional. As a body, it was extremely uneven in quality.

Classical plays performed professionally and new plays performed by amateurs characterize the early history of the movement, and it seems that the revival of interest in religious drama of the past inspired amateurs to write and produce their own less demanding short plays. William Poel's seminal production of *Everyman* (1901) stimulated professional interest in performing early Renaissance and medieval works. Nugent Monck founded the Norwich Players to specialize in medieval drama at the Maddermarket Theatre, Norwich. These morality plays, as they were generally known, inspired the pre–World War I amateur Morality Play Society.

These totally amateur efforts seldom resulted in anything remarkable. Successful plays with contemporary impact in production and that have surviving interest as texts and/or productions usually were those of writers, directors, and actors who had established reputations and experience. Also, these survivors were associated with more sizable and important occasions and venues. Economically organizers of big festivals were anxious to choose a play that would win audiences and justify the trouble taken, and usually the raising of money for religious purposes was a factor (a major factor if urgent church repairs were needed, a minor factor even if centenary celebrations were the immediate pretext). And large audiences and prestige attracted talented writers and casts where an obscure village hall did not. Naturally, few were as unworldly as Gordon Bottomley, who was simply interested in having his plays performed by anyone anywhere. The exceptions to this rule occurred when a dramatist was willing to write a play for an obscure village hall because he lived in the local community, as did Christopher Fry with *The Boy with a Cart*. Thus, for a small provincial production, the average play was written for a specific occasion by a willing amateur.

One benefit of the religious drama movement was that it could extend its conventions further than the other well-delimited categories of play at that time. Because of modern wide definitions of drama and interest in paradramatic events, we are less likely to dismiss either village or cathedral performances because many of them do not produce a text as artwork to join the literary canon. The motives and appreciation of audiences of the parish church nativity play, then and now, combine directly religious response to the church celebration, a satisfactory sense of participation in social tradition, interest in observing known neighbors in novel activities, and several other community aspects. To the village audience, spectacle, poetry, character, and the rest of Aristotle's tragic elements are certainly no more important than these community reactions, if as important. Similarly, T. S. Eliot suspected that the religious festival audience in the larger towns was equally unlikely to be assessing the religious festival play on its merits. But this attention in itself could mean a paradoxical expectation or tolerance of something dramatically unusual, such as a chorus, intervention into the auditorium, song, or verse—unusual outside the more progressive theaters in London.

In practice, however, this did not provide the stimulus to mainstream commercial drama that it might have because, as Eliot had predicted, expectations were compartmentalized, and what was acceptable in Canterbury Cathedral was rarely acceptable on the West End stage. But it did mean that the commissioning of plays was more adventurous in the less commercial festival circuit. For instance, the Glastonbury Festival pioneered a "new plays" approach and asked A. E. Housman to write a play (*Bethlehem*) in 1922. The vigorous expansion in religious drama production began in 1928 at Canterbury. George Bell, dean of Canterbury and immensely influential in the movement's development, was responsible for the production of John Masefield's play, *The Coming of Christ*, in 1928. This was successful enough to lead to the first formal annual festival the next year, when *Everyman* was played at the Cathedral West door and *Dr. Faustus* in the chapter house. Most important, the Religious Drama Society was founded.

Evidently George Bell had a strong and proselytizing sense of the importance of drama to religion; he lent his name to the new society as president. But he was, after all, a clergyman, not an impresario or, far less, a director, and his influence operated mainly indirectly—by inspiring and enabling others to work. He moved to become bishop of Chichester and at once set up the position of director of religious drama in his new diocese, appointing E. Martin Browne to fulfill this role. Bell was skillful in bringing writers together and involving them in his plans; both T. S. Eliot and Gordon Bottomley recall gatherings designed to coax them to write for the movement. He also followed the activities in his own neighborhood; he attended the little village production of Fry's *The Boy with a Cart* and had it presented again in the garden of the Bishop's Palace in Chichester the following year.

E. Martin Browne was perhaps best known as T. S. Eliot's director, but he also influenced the careers of several other playwrights. Having discovered Fry as a promising writer in the Chichester diocese, Browne encouraged him with the commission to write a play for the Tewkesbury Festival. After the war he asked Fry to contribute to a season of plays—in verse but not necessarily religious—that he was putting on in London. During the war, when entertainment was scarce and not very accessible, Browne had taken a tiny touring company around village halls and schools putting on mainly religious plays. But in 1947 he decided to put on this season of plays in verse at the small Mercury Theatre in Notting Hill, London, and this was to involve Fry further in the poetic drama movement.

Poetic Drama

E. Martin Browne's poetic drama season was not specifically for religious drama writers, but the fact that most of the contributing dramatists did produce works with a religious theme (and Fry's play, *A Phoenix Too Frequent*, though the most secular, also deals with change, redemption, death, and new life) shows how important the religious drama movement had been in accustoming writers and audiences to verse plays. T. S. Eliot was inevitably a dominating figure; not only had *Murder in the Cathedral* been successful, but by this time he had also written *The Family Reunion* (1939) as an attempt to use verse for a drama on the lines of the modern problem play. Its effect confused audiences—the theme of expiation was not explicit, and it used silent apparitions of the Eumenides rather than Christian imagery—and it did not have a long run, but the challenge was clear: modern drama could include plays in verse, and these could be produced in secular theaters as well as in abbey ruins in the provinces.

As with the religious drama movement, some initiatives in writing verse plays are apparent from the beginning of the century, with the much-hailed but now little-read works by Stephen Phillips and Laurence Binyon, as well as the surviving major plays by William B. Yeats and, later, W. H. Auden and Christopher Isherwood. Yeats and Eliot wrote crusading statements about the importance of extending the language of drama to regain the variety and flexibility they felt had been lost in realistic plays, and during the forties and fifties, it was mainly Eliot's and Fry's plays that seemed to show the feasibility of modern poetic drama. After this, the play wholly in verse grew scarce again, though a widening of theatrical conventions meant that verse and song were used in plays along with other nonnaturalistic devices.

At the time Fry was writing, however, Eliot was struggling to recolonize drama for poetry, believing, as he later wrote, that drama, like all other great literature, should deal with values and moral judgments, particularly "the primacy of the supernatural over the natural life," as presented through the predicaments and reactions that human beings suffer because of these values and judgments.[1] Poetry could best present this often complex subject matter, "the frontiers of consciousness beyond which words fail though meanings still exist."[2] He had also reasoned that blank verse could no longer be used for drama, partly because "its rhythms had become too remote from the movement of modern speech."[3] Like many other critics, Eliot thought that previous attempts to revive poetic drama to a semblance of its importance in Shakespeare's day had foundered because of too much imitation of a long-dead Shakespearean style. He saw the problem as one of uniting poetry with the movement of modern speech in order to bring out "the contemporary relevance of the situation."[4] Historical subjects, then, were a kind of cheating, because "picturesque period costume renders verse much more acceptable."[5] Similarly, religious festival plays were not a good example of uniting poetry and contemporary relevance; they were usually in period costume and presented to the public as "a kind of poetry recital which it does them credit to enjoy," not as serious plays that stand or fall by their dramatic merits.[6] Thus, he concluded, "people are prepared to put up with verse from the lips of personages dressed in the fashion of some distant age; they should be made to hear it from people dressed like ourselves, living in houses and apartments like ours, and using telephones and motor cars and radio sets."[7] Here, as in his conviction that the texture of the verse should be unobtrusive—"the effect

. . . should be unconscious"—Eliot shows differences with, as well as similarities to, Fry's views.[8]

Certainly both Eliot and Fry agreed that poetry penetrated to the truth beneath the blurred communication of everyday speech. Eliot said: "A verse play is not a play done into verse, but a different kind of play: in a way more realistic than 'naturalistic drama,' because instead of clothing nature in poetry, it should remove the surface of things, expose the underneath or the inside of the natural surface appearance."[9] Fry noted that in naturalistic drama, "we have gained verisimilitude but we have lost truth"; if, for example, in a naturalistic play, we have an anxious heroine awaiting her lover, "What, in common speech, she would say is something like 'Oh do, do, *do* come back quickly, John!' It is not a very adequate demonstration of what her whole being is *really* saying."[10] Essentially both writers see poetic drama as expressing this "what her whole being is *really* saying." But Fry has fewer misgivings than Eliot about what an audience would be prepared to accept:

The overemphasis nowadays on being "contemporary" is meaningless. Telephones, trousers, neuroses; nymphomania and dipsomania: are supposed to hold a special message for our times. . . . The period, (except in a strictly historical play) is merely the colour on the brush: the extra illumination of the idea. I do not believe that audiences as a whole disassociate themselves because the clothes on the characters on stage are different from the clothes on their backs, so long as thought and language are contemporary. Neither do I think the audiences have any difficulty in accepting poetry as the natural idiom of a play which is dressed and housed in the current fashion. ("Poetry and the Theatre," 8)

Although Fry quoted Eliot's views on the effect of verse being "unconscious" and added, "This we would all agree with," the language of his own plays is quite definitely not of an unnoticed and unconscious operation, and indeed he went on to say that "there is no need to do it by stealth." Possibly because of his experience with different kinds of audiences, Fry had the confidence to continue to write dialogue of a recognizably poetic kind in both his early religious festival plays and the comedies that made his reputation.

The Boy with a Cart

Fry's first play to be published, and one he has a particular affection for, is *The Boy with a Cart*. He claims to suffer perennial difficulty in getting plot outlines, the germ of a play, and the subject of *The Boy with a Cart* was suggested by the vicar of Coleman's Hatch in Sussex, who knew Fry was a dramatist and wanted to put on a play in the village. The central character, Cuthman, was a local saint. Though a native of Cornwall, his long migration to the Sussex village of Steyning and his founding of a little church there qualified him as a "Sussex worthy."

Briefly, the play describes how the youthful Cuthman, a shepherd boy, on his father's death, sets off on a new life trusting in the guidance of God and taking with him his old widowed mother whom he pulled in a cart he had made himself. He is not seeking his fortune in the opportunistic way of folk-tales but has an inner confidence, that this is God's will for him. Three miracles mark Cuthman's career. First, when the cart's harness rope breaks, peasant mowers who laugh and jeer at him are punished by a neatly localized downpour—just enough to ruin their crop. The second miracle also involves weather control, as Cuthman, settled at last in the village of Steyning and setting about the inspired task of building its first church, is hindered by the bad-tempered Fipps family. Mrs. Fipps is bodily whirled away by a tornado while her two sons stand stupefied in the harness of the oxen they have stolen from Cuthman. These miracles are negative (though defensive), but the third divine intervention is constructive: the wooden church built by the villagers is almost finished, but the fall of the king beam, immovable by the unskilled peasants, threatens to frustrate their achievement. Cuthman interrupts the lamentations to tell his neighbors that, off-stage, his prayers have been answered by the appearance of a shining figure who with a gesture has moved the colossal beam back into position.

The dramatization, Fry says, was shaped by the elements of the story. The emblem of the cart and the journey too suggested an episodic structure. Within the series of hagiographic events, however, much space is spent on setting up the situation and characters, giving a leisurely start and a brisk conclusion. Each miracle episode has its own self-contained structure: tension, reversal, release. Each is short as well as crisp, and each tends to get shorter. The last miracle, because its resolution is offstage and narrated, is briefest of all, and this increases the pace of the play overall, a movement to which the chorus contributes. The chorus of the People of the South of England, supplemented by a subchorus of neighbors in both Cornwall and Sussex, extends the early scenes with comment and description and telescopes the time scheme of the later scenes by bridging long narrative intervals.

It is important to establish Cuthman's character and the world he moves in at an early stage because, as in Fry's later plays, the mainly comic events have significance only within the framework of the characters and their worlds. A picaresque tale has a different meaning according to whether the adventurer is Don Quixote, Tom Jones, or Cuthman of Sussex. The discomfiture of the

mowers and the Fippses reinforces Cuthman's reliance on God to bring
wrong to a good end. The effect is more than mere points scoring over the
villains because more than a quarter of the play has been concerned with
Cuthman's role in a purposeful God-guided scheme of things, and this
purposefulness—rather than other possible epistemological systems such as
humanism or realism—is thus signified by Cuthman's little victories.

Cuthman is less like the tormented martyrs of the early church and more
like the characters from the Old Testament, such as Tobias or Jonah, but
without the ominous threat of God's wrath. The play as a whole becomes a
paradigm of stable, secure human life. Its center of gravity is the careful
coupling of God's hand, and the destructiveness of people and nature is sub-
ordinate to this:

> Despite the jibbing, man destroying, denying,
> Disputing, or the late frost looting the land
> Of green. Despite flood and the lightning's rifle
> In root and sky we can discern the hand.
>
> (1:8)

Cuthman's worst afflictions are the sudden death of his father and the disaster that attacks his nearly completed church; the former is accepted, the latter remedied, and there is never any sense of evil, of precariousness, much less
of a universe sliding into chaos and godless savagery as in Eliot's religious
plays. Loss and pain do not damage Cuthman's innocent confidence, though
the chorus suggests the possibility: "How is your faith now, Cuthman . . . can
faith for long elude / Prevailing fever?" (1:14). This pain serves to modify
"the green recklessness of little knowledge" (1:14). Cuthman realizes he
needs to achieve a more mature acceptance of a world that is less simple than
he thought, but on the whole the friendly neighbors outnumber the hostile
ones, and good fortune far outweighs bad. In this little play, then, the "perspective of the vision" (1:16) directs us to see Cuthman in terms of his place
in God's plan, and his confidence and good humor as signs of his right response to that plan, not as individual character qualities that are significant in
the action.

The particularly joyful, unstressed atmosphere of *The Boy with a Cart*
derives from this lack of conflict. Cuthman and God's plan are in harmony,
and in spite of an early bereavement, Cuthman carries his innocence into the
world of experience, not so much because he hands over responsibility to
God but because he never doubts, either God or himself. As the title says,
Cuthman is a boy (though a picture of him in York Minster shows him as a

bearded peasant with a barrow), and the everyday miracle that he has been able to effect before the play opens—to draw an invisible circle around his sheep that, with a prayer, pens them as effectively as a fence—is a boy's miracle, a kind of blessed harmony with the nature of things. But after his first sorrow has precipitated him on his pilgrimage as a wiser though not less innocent pilgrim, miracles are made for him as signs of grace.

The comparatively long opening sequence gives a philosophical and atmospheric basis to the play as Cuthman echoes the chorus's unifying faith. His reaction to the blows of his father's death and the family's sudden destitution is a mixture of faith in God and a new plan, made concrete in the material form of his homemade cart. Structurally the fall of the king post in the last episode balances the death of his father at the beginning. Like his father's death, it has a profound effect on his faith and temporarily shakes his innocent confidence: "now he has gone into a ghost," says a neighbor, and "this will damage him" (1:44), says his mother.

This time Cuthman is not left to struggle with disaster. He has had to accept the shadowy side of the human lot before, but this last miracle raises his experience above mere acceptance or fatalism. As a saint, Cuthman exemplifies a life made purposeful by God's will, and his purpose is fulfilled to justify his faith. He had said, "The church / And I shall be built together; and together / Find our significance" (1:28), and the repositioning of the king post indicates the deeper working of God beneath the fluctuating events of human life.

Cuthman perceives the power of God through mystic experience too. The People of the South of England have an intuition of the presence of God in their daily lives, but Cuthman's experience is direct. At first his sense of unity with his surroundings is an intensification of the chorus's assurances and accompanies his sheep-penning miracle: "I was suddenly filled with faith— Suddenly parcelled with faith like a little wain / In a good hay season" (1:10). His next inspiration is more overwhelming. While the jeering mowers are being rained off, Cuthman feels a change in the very texture of reality:

> I felt the mood
> Of the meadow change, as though a tide
> Had turned in the sap, or heaven from the balance
> Of creation had shifted a degree.
> The skirling water crept into a flow,
> The sapling flickered in my hand, timber
> And flesh seemed of equal and old significance.
> At that place, and then, I tell you, Mother,

> God rode up my spirit and drew in
> Beside me. His breath met on my breath, moved
> And mingled. I was taller then than death.
> Under the willows I was taller than death.
>
> (1:27)

Cuthman now suddenly knows that his destiny is to build a church at the place where his new cart harness, a withy rope, will break. The culminating experience of the play is the appearance of Christ to Cuthman as the figure who says, "I was a Carpenter." This figure is seen in terms of sunlight and gold but also with an intense stillness that again raises the experience beyond the natural: "So still that the air seemed to leap / At his side" (1:44). This is a different dimension from the pastoral beauty, however great, of the world the characters normally move in.

In this play, the beauty of the natural world is emphasized and, like Cuthman's innocence, creates a harmony strikingly in contrast with the misery of T. S. Eliot's chorus of later medieval people in *Murder in the Cathedral*. The scope and aim of *Murder* as a long tragedy for a big public festival is, of course, not the same as *The Boy with a Cart,* a short comedy for a local celebration, but the contrast is all the more evident because of the noticeable Eliotian influence on Fry's choral verse here. This influence appears particularly in the rhythm of the speeches, though the vocabulary used is quite different; Fry aims to evoke pleasant images where Eliot is seeking unpleasant ones. For instance, in the opening chorus, the People of the South of England are positing a generous, beautiful, natural world in which human beings play their part sustained by a sense of unity and reliance on God; people perceive this unity within and through the nature and cycle of their agricultural labors:

> we have felt
> Heaven ride with Spring into the meadows.
>
> We have felt the joint action of root and sky, of man
> And God, when day first risks the hills, and when
> The darkness hangs the hatchet in the barn
> And scrapes the heavy boot against the iron . . .
>
> Coming out from our doorways on October nights
> We have seen the sky unfreeze and a star drip

> Into the south: experienced alteration
> Beyond experience.

                                        (1:8)

In Eliot's opening chorus, similar elements—roots, land, spring, October
—are placed in a different set of associations and bring not beauty, unity, and
mystic insight but decay and despair; nature is heavily material and drags humanity away from spiritual salvation:

> Since golden October declined into sombre November
> And the apples were gathered and stored, and the land became
> brown sharp points of death in a waste of water and mud,
> The New Year waits, breathes, waits, whispers in darkness.
> While the labourer kicks off a muddy boot and stretches his
> hand to the fire . . .
>
>   and who shall
> Stretch out his hand to the fire, and deny his master? . . .
>
> Ruinous Spring shall beat at our doors,
> Root and shoot shall eat our eyes and our ears.
> Disastrous summer burn up the beds of our streams
> And the poor shall wait for another decaying October.[11]

It is surprising, then, to find echoes of Eliotian rhythms overriding Fry's
idyllic content—rhythms that are particularly evident when the play is performed because they are shaped by the speech rhythms rather than formal
versification (not that the versification is in either case very formal). In fact
Fry and Eliot are using a flexible verse form, which looks quite different in
print. Fry's verse paragraphs are made up of lines of a fairly even length with
five main stresses and a variable number of unstressed syllables; Eliot's choruses (unlike the four-stressed staple dialogue of the play) are much more uneven, as in "And the labourer bends to his piece of earth, earth-colour, his own
colour. / Preferring to pass unobserved."[12] This flexibility means that the
unit of meaning is the phrase or clause with its own internal rhythm of the
natural strong and weak stresses, unmodified by regular metric pattern. And
although Eliot in *Murder* is using a far more varied range of speech rhythms,
questions, statements, repetitions, and so on, as is evident in the brief sections
quoted, there are some recurrent characteristic patterns that are recognizable
and also appear in *The Boy with a Cart*.

Both Fry's and Eliot's choruses are expressing their habitual lives and re-

cent experiences, which, though different in content, tend to require the same
verb tenses and participles. Nevertheless, the audience immediately recognizes the hesitating, repetitive, modifying expression of ideas as the actors'
voices swoop through a series of unfinished cadences until the ideas are allowed to rest. This circling movement appears in the following lines from *The
Boy with a Cart*:

> Not knowing yet and yet sometimes discerning:
> Discerning a little at Spring where the bud and shoot
> With pointing fingers show the hand at the root,
> With stretching finger point the mood in the sky.
>
>   (1:7)

They are like Eliot's

>   . . . not in the hands of statesmen
> Who do, some well, some ill, planning and guessing,
> Having their aims which turn in their hands in the pattern of
> time.[13]

Fry's

>   or at the end
> Of a furrow, watching the lark dissolve in sun,
> We have almost known, a little have known
> The work that is with our work.
>
>   (1:8)

is like Eliot's

> Are afraid in a fear which we cannot know, which we cannot face,
> which none understands,
> And our hearts are torn from us, our brains unskinned like the
> layers of an onion, ourselves are lost lost.[14]

Although the sunlit lark and the onion-skinned brain contrast, the modifica-
tions of knowing and fearing are repeated in similar half-line phrases. Much
of the similarity depends on the pattern of definite article plus abstract noun
plus *of* plus abstract noun. This is obvious in the more similar subject matter
of Fry's

> Out of this, out of the first incision
> Of mortality on mortality, there comes
> The genuflexion, and the partition of pain
> Between man and God.
>
> (1:16)

and Eliot's

> Who fear the blessing of God, the loneliness of the night of God,
> the surrender required, the deprivation inflicted;
> Who fear the injustice of men less than the justice of God.[15]

The subject matter of *The Boy with a Cart* has more in common with Eliot's *The Rock* and Fry's own *The Tower* in that it has the positive motive and theme of building, and like *The Rock* it takes in a great variety of writing styles—perhaps experimentally; Fry says that he later rejected variety and sought for a single verse style that "would do for everything." At one end of the scale are the choral speeches, Cuthman's soliloquies, and some of his dialogue. These are formal, complex, image packed, and sometimes rhymed. At the other extreme, Cuthman's mother's address to the audience is a rambling familiar prose: "Well, I must now draw to a close. I have some milk on the fire and by this time it will probably all be boiled over" (1:37). Cuthman speaks not only in verse but also in a functional prose—"I'm sorry they were trespassing. I'll see in future that they stay where they belong. If you could fetch them for me I'll put them to work" (1:38)—and in a more rhetorical prose—"There's one thing that I'll not see any man destroy; there's one fire that no man shall put out" (1:38). Most of the villagers speak in prose when not performing a choral function. Mrs. Fipps at one point begins a tirade in verse and continues it in prose. There is no apology or awkwardness about the transitions between these styles; the characters move from one to another, and in performance this works perfectly.

Critical reaction to Fry's later plays complained of the looseness of his metric form and questioned whether lines of such unobtrusive rhythm qualified as poetry. It is true that in *The Boy with a Cart* Fry is already using the loose five-stress line as his staple form, but he occasionally emphasizes rhythmic control in specific passages, as where, paradoxically, the irregular rhythm is supposedly imitating an irregular tune, which in turn is an image for the play's elliptic time scheme:

> Do you catch the time of the tune that the shepherd plays
> Under the irregular bough of the oak-tree,
> The tune of the tale he expects your brain to dance to,
> The time of the tune irregular as the bough?
>
> (1:42)

There is no doubt that Fry is capable of achieving complex effects with rhythm, but he preferred on the whole not to make such effects. Usually there is only an indication that the lines are varied in length when those lines happen to rhyme. Many of Fry's rhymes are half-rhymes and assonances, so this indication is not always strong, but in the opening chorus, for instance, the couplets are close and regular enough for the pattern to be remarked by ear, and the change is noticeable when alternate stanzas move to an alternate line rhyme scheme. On the other hand, the ear is unlikely to pick up the most complex pattern in the choral speech, "For the lifetime of a sapling-rope" (1:29), which goes *a b c c a b d d e f g g,* with its elusive assonances of "twine, strain" in the couplets and firmer rhymes five lines apart. In spite of the wide variety of styles, then, and the complexity that is evident to readers, Fry, as in his later less varied plays, is relying for the main effect of his verse on the lexical and semantic impact, in the way the vocabulary and its connotations strike his audience; rhythm and rhyme are secondary.

The use of a chorus was common in a religious poetic drama at this time. Here it has the traditional functions of giving information about the background and progress of the plot, setting the scene, describing offstage action, and commenting philosophically on the implications of events as they arise. Eliot says that the use of a chorus was an easy way for him to deal with such dramatic problems, but in *The Boy with a Cart* it was not particularly an advantage for Fry to give off these functions to the chorus because he was not concerned to keep his dialogue free from philosophy or explanation. Why, apart from convention, use a chorus at all? It adds another, sometimes intentionally anachronistic, level of commentary, which enriches the texture and reinforces the episodic organization of the play. Structurally Fry uses the chorus to divide the episodes of Cuthman's life, as well as to control the pace. Having introduced Cuthman, the chorus recedes to allow the scene to take place between him and the neighbors, who tell him of his father's death. After the neighbors have gone, the chorus speaks its lyrical stanzas alternately with Cuthman's unrhymed soliloquies so that Cuthman's straightforward lamentations are confronted with the wider problem of pain. The chorus hints at the possibility, rejected by Cuthman, that suffering could cause a rebellion against a God who had permitted it.

Fry is able to use the chorus's wider viewpoint in evaluating implications of events and by offering an overview of the life of Cuthman; it thus reflects the unity that is the theme of the play. The chorus is the People of the South of England, with a collective experience of mowing and sowing and so on. From the first, it emphasizes the way Cuthman is to find the meaning of his life in doing as God wills—not as a martyr in conflict with circumstances but by channeling the natural powers and purpose of himself and his fellows. Therefore, they express not only the experience of humanity but the presence of the natural world in its reassuring agricultural routine, its impersonal beauty, and its embodiment of God's hidden purpose and control. It speaks for man and nature. Hence the pervasive idyllic natural descriptions and the similar imagery that relates abstractions to nature too: "We pull / Down weeks and months like a bough of cherry. (1:36) . . . Cuthman's life is puffed like a dandelion / Into uncertain places" (1:45).

The Cuthman story is a simple one. The minimal conflict in the saint's progress demands little complexity of characterization. The mowers and the Fippses are naturally uncooperative and malicious, as Cuthman's mother is naturally voluble and concerned about her respectability, complaining in the tradition of Mrs. Noah; but she is not blindly intransigent. Rather, she is caught between faith and caution and defends her son stoutly against outsiders. This part adds to the comedy of the play, as does that of Tawm, the Sussex elder who is eccentric in trying to escape from his loving family's irksome cosseting. The broad characterization and the humor, like the optimistic and appreciative pastoral atmosphere, is fitted for the amateur village festival for which the play was written.

Cuthman, though straightforward in his development from confidence to acceptance, has more depth to his character. He is destined to go beneath the practical problems to a direct perception of the presence and control of God. On the other hand, his linguistic agility seems to show not only special perceptiveness but also a surprising sophistication. It is a convention of poetic drama (and of much prose drama) that everyone is unusually articulate. Audiences probably have little clear idea of how a dramatist "ought" to make an eleventh-century shepherd speak, but Cuthman's "chancelled larches / Sing like Lenten choirboys, a green treble" (1:9) and "earth / Tossed its tentative hills" (1:35) suggest a particularly surprising articulacy in the lucid, single-minded boy with a cart (a discrepancy Fry does not introduce into his last saint play about the inspired stable man Caedmon).

As a first play, or at least a first published play, *The Boy with a Cart* gave a paradigm of what Fry could do. The structure, set, and characterization are suited to the limitations of the amateur company, and there are signs of dramatic flexibility in the assured use of chorus and climactic effects like the whirlwind (even if this has to be economically mimed rather than presented through spectacular staging). Most significant is the range of dramatic writing. Both the Eliotian influence and the frequent changes of style are elements Fry could have developed further. He did not. Like Eliot, Fry next pursued the ideal of a verse that would do for everything, and, after the sunny optimism of *The Boy with a Cart,* he started work on a tragedy.

Chapter Three

Early Religious Plays:
The Firstborn and
Thor, with Angels

The Firstborn

Fry has said that when he writes a comedy, the idea comes to him first in terms of tragedy, but *The Firstborn* is one play that remained a tragedy. Comedy would not have been impossible, but given this subject—the story of Moses' efforts to release the Israelites from Egyptian bondage—comedy would have to be harsh and farcical to smoothe over the mass deaths on both Jewish and Egyptian sides.

The biblical story tells how Moses demands that the Egyptian pharaoh permit the departure of the huge numbers of Israelites settled in Egypt, where they are subjected to slave labor enforced by cruelty. Pharaoh's refusal is punished by divine plagues, the first being the turning of the Nile waters into blood. Thereafter, there is a repetition of the pattern of Pharaoh's capitulation and agreement, the withdrawal of the plague, Pharaoh's change of mind, and the infliction of a new plague. Ten plagues are visited upon the increasingly resentful Egyptian population, and after the tenth plague, the Israelites are at last allowed to leave. (Pharaoh's further rethinking and pursuit of the Israelites into the Red Sea is not part of Fry's play.)

In the Bible, the life of Moses the prophet offers much potential for dramatic treatment. One of the best-known images is of the aged Moses receiving the Ten Commandments on tablets of stone on Mount Sinai; another is of his sister Miriam hiding the newborn Moses from the massacre of Jewish babies in a floating basket among the bulrushes of the Nile, where he was found and adopted by Pharaoh's daughter. Fry chooses to concentrate only on Moses' rescue of his people from bondage, ignoring the later lawgiving sequence and including the bulrushes story as a brief expositional reminiscence by Pharaoh's daughter, Anath. The emphasis is not on the charm and warmth of the baby's rescue but on the consequences for Moses the adult: he has thereby become an alien to his own race and to his adopted race, trying to expiate his period of privilege and indifference.

In Exodus, Pharaoh's stubbornness and repeated humiliations are more exemplary than realistic, and both these humiliations and the well-deserved but less lethal plagues, such as frogs and lice, could be made funny enough by a comic dramatist, with the ultimate triumph of right and the victimized Israelites giving a happy ending. But comedy would have a harder problem with the sufferings of the Jews, including the forced labor and the infanticide of male babies, and the Egyptians also suffer many plagues that are not as temporary in effect as frogs and lice, such as the death of the cattle and the extermination of their firstborn sons. Thus the Pharaoh in *The Firstborn*, Seti II, is subject to the classic tragic humbling of pride and fall from prosperity when his own son, Rameses, the firstborn of the title, dies in the last divine plague. And though the biblical story stresses the triumph of the Israelites, Fry's play gives equal weight to the sufferings of both sides. The suffering has been so far in excess of the result that Fry's Moses accepts the release not vindictively but tragically.

No questioning of divine destructiveness appears in the biblical original. Exodus is presenting an indictment of Egyptian persecution from the victims' point of view and says of Pharaoh's obstinacy in withdrawing permission to leave as soon as each plague subsides that "God hardened Pharaoh's heart."[1] Pharaoh both deserved and was controlled in deserving his own doom, and so Exodus justifies the ways of God to man. *The Firstborn* expands the human dimension without excluding the influence of God. God may be hardening Pharaoh Seti's heart, but Seti does not know this, and we find what motives—political, economic, and psychological—he and the other characters think they have, as they do the acts enforced by God. We come to understand the feelings of Seti, of Princess Anath, once Moses' foster mother and now embittered by his alienation, of young Rameses, idealistic, affectionate, determined to restore the Israelites to freedom and dignity when he is pharaoh. The plagues that afflict these Egyptians have as much importance for us as the persecutions of the Israelites.

Although Moses is said in Exodus to be four score years old at this return to Egypt, Fry makes him merely a mature adult and also a military commander whose exile has interrupted a military career of genius. This genius is the reason for Pharaoh's desire to win him back to Egypt's service. Seti II is not the same pharaoh whose decree the baby Moses so narrowly escaped but his son, and therefore not an old man but a middle-aged ruler, nearer Moses' age. These adjustments and additions give the play a specifically military and political focus: men of military age are dealing, among other things, with politico-military conditions.

Fry began *The Firstborn* in 1938, worked at it on and off during World War II, and finished it in 1946. The experiences of these years shaped the direction of the play. The conflicts and stresses of wartime are reflected in the concerns of Pharaoh's kingdom; the persecution of the Israelites refers to the sufferings of the Jews during World War II. Fry's memory, however, is that in the thirties and forties, the magnitude of this suffering was only slowly recognized, and the numbers of those killed by Pharaoh's overseers, though appropriate to the size of a task force working on the large but limited imperial enterprise, are trivial in relation to the six million killed by the Nazis, revealed after the war. Moreover, the scale of the original story did not allow a recasting of Egyptian persecutions to parallel modern atrocities as recognition of these developed.

Thus the implications of modern man's inhumanity to man, and the place of God in permitting it, are implicit in the play, which nevertheless strains a little to accommodate the issue. At the same time, the attempt to explain Seti's behavior necessarily presents him too as a victim. The play has to become the expression of a complex and tortuous historical event, of the role of human beings in history when the process is seen as directed by God. This issue, Fry later admitted, was not fully realized in the play, and the problem was partly one of dramatic structure. The whole play had delicately led up to Moses' realization of his God's destructiveness and left too little time for him to deal with the challenge.

The Firstborn is structurally much more sophisticated than *The Boy with a Cart*; the ten plagues do not dictate a ten-scene episodic sequence, with all the problems of repetition that that would pose. The play opens on the terrace of Seti's palace, overlooking the unfinished pyramid, where the Israelite masses are being forced to work, out of sight. Pharaoh's sister Anath and his young daughter Teusret appear on the terrace, alarmed by the first sound we have heard, a scream. A guard tells them it was only another Israelite falling to his death. This ominous sequence is crucial for the play; it not only sets up a pressure toward the ultimate release and restitution to the Israelites but also establishes the atmosphere—this is a play pervaded by death. The dramatic opening leads to an equally dramatic entrance for Moses: Seti asks Anath where Moses, whom they have not seen for ten years, is now living in self-imposed exile; hardly has Rameses interrupted with a question about a tall foreigner he has seen than the foreigner enters, and he is Moses.

Moses is to bring a new life to his people; he is also to bring much death. He is an intense, preoccupied figure. Death had caused Moses' flight—he had killed a brutal Egyptian overseer who was beating a Jew—and the deaths of the Israelite multitudes have brought him back. Accusatory from the first, he has heard "my blood weeping" (1:67) and is in no mood to meet Pharaoh's overtures of reconciliation. Seti's motive is his need to wipe out the threatening Libyan army. Moses is absolute in his demands: the Israelites' freedom is a right he insists they must have without his compromising or making any concessions for it. Young Rameses, however, vibrant with life, wants to compromise; he persuades Seti to make Miriam's son, Moses' nephew Shendi, an officer in the Egyptian army as a gesture of good faith, but the value of this gesture is set against Moses' entrance bearing the body of a Jewish child killed by the overseers. Repeatedly in the play, a movement or feeling of hope is juxtaposed with an immediate blow.

Seti is decently regretful but excuses this death and all of the other Israelite deaths as inevitable: "Blame, dear Moses, / The gods for their creative plan which is / Not to count the cost but enormously / To bring about" (1:95). Moses contemptuously rejects the narrowness and destructiveness of the Egyptian gods, but his assertion of his own God introduces another and equally destructive phase of the conflict. Moses defies Pharaoh with an appeal to the dead:

> I am here by fury and the heart. Is that not
> A law? I am here to appease the unconsummated
> Resourceless dead, to join life to the living.
> Is that not underwritten by nature? Is that
> Not a law? Do not ask me why I do it!
> I live. I do this thing. I was born this action.
> Despite you, through you, upon you,
> I am compelled.
>
> (1:96)

The act ends with an ominous supernatural thunder following his speech; his God sounds no less ruthless than those of the Egyptians.

The thunder suggests that control of events has been taken out of human hands. The next act begins with the first plague, unexpected and unannounced in its horror—the turning of water into blood. Moses is making practical plans, ignoring Aaron's premonitions, until Miriam's half-hysterical entry with news of blood spreading unnaturally from the Nile transforms the situation from pragmatic guerrilla warfare to a holy war. Evidence of Rameses' goodwill, in Shendi's commission as an officer, and Anath's message that Seti has conceded Moses' demands seem signs of rationalism and hope, but the divine force making for the Israelites' release is more massive and more ruthless.

This marks the beginning of a new structural phase; the blood is the first of the signs of divine intervention. The Egyptians are not allowed to escape through compromises, and the Israelites are not allowed to escape through their own efforts. Death matches death; the characters can only react. Evidently the bloodless solutions Rameses and Anath proposed are ironic, as blood flows from well and river. Miriam's uneasy "How could the water be blood, Shendi?" (1:106) is ignored by her son but undermines the hopeful departures of Moses and Shendi. There is no formal interval before the next scene, but the juxtaposition of Anath's weary, shattered speech, recounting the devastation of the plagues, effectively eliminates any fragile hopes that survived the previous scene:

> I looked out, and when I looked to the north I saw
> Instead of quiet cattle, glutted jackals,
> Not trees and pasture but vulture-bearing boughs
> And fields which had been sown with hail. And looking
> To the south I saw, like falling ashes after fire,
> Death after thirst, death after hunger, death
> After disease.
>
> (1:107)

The dramatic shock is evident: prosperous Egypt is brought low. Anath continues to enumerate the effects of the plagues and bitterly points out that Seti's broken promises to Moses have led to this, a blame he rejects as "superstition." The struggle is still going on as Anath is aghast to hear that Seti has reneged on his promise yet again. Incidental to this confrontation between Seti and Moses, Rameses suffers the first serious disillusion to his youthful idealism, witnessing the officer Shendi ill-treating his own people as brutally as the Egyptians do. But it is Anath who questions not only Seti's breaking the rules of the game but the whole divine game itself:

> What is this divinity
> Which with no more dexterity than a man
> Rips up good things to make a different kind
> Of good?
>
> (1:119)

Moses admits that his God is now as destructive as that of her people; the God of the Hebrews "lets all go, lets all waste and go, / Except, dearly retained in his palm, the soul" (1:118). Here act 2 ends with the ninth plague, as frightening and prophetic as the first; the plague of darkness blackens the stage before the curtain falls, leaving us with only the voices of the characters.

The action has been moving toward the destructive climax of act 3. The efforts of Aaron, Anath, and Rameses toward civilized negotiation have been no more than gestures, soon crushed. The last act opens with the dark ritual of Passover. More blood, lamb's blood, has been daubed three times over the entrance of every Israelite tent in uncomprehending obedience to Moses's orders. There is a sense of immanent presence in the surroundings: "The night is dedicated to our cause" (1:123). Moses reveals the prophecy to Aaron, Miriam, and Shendi:

> Tonight, at midnight,
> God will unfasten the hawk of death from his
> Grave wrist, to let it rake our world,
> Descend and obliterate the firstborn of Egypt,
> All the firstborn, cattle, flocks, and men:
> Mortality lunging in the midnight fields
> And briding in the beds: a sombre visit
> Such as no nation has known before.
>
> (1:127)

Aaron sees at once that the firstborn must include Rameses, a fact that Moses has not realized and recognizes now with a dreadful shock, desperately arguing, "When other boys were slaughtered I was spared for Israel. / Surely I who have been the go-between for God / Can keep one firstborn living now for Egypt?" (1:128). It is not the first time that Moses has been vividly confronted by the pain of the "necessary deaths" argument. Reiterating it, Aaron reminds him of the many other youths who died in his armies and of the dead Israelite child who earlier evoked his rejection of Seti's excuse. But here the necessary death is that of both an enemy and a friend. Ironically the plight of Rameses, the generous enemy, is juxtaposed with that of the weak, brutalized Shendi, who has claimed identity with the doomed Egyptian conquerors. The inexorable deity eliminates both youths. Shendi leaves the tent briefly but long enough to be smitten by the wings of the destroying angel that passes over at midnight: "Let me go, death; death let me go!" (1:130). And when he repents, it is too late: he staggers out crying useless reproaches after the destroyer: "Only free to die? / This wasn't a world. It was death from the beginning" (1:131). Similarly Moses tries in vain to save Rameses: "We'll hold you with our lives if our lives will hold" (1:137). But Anath is bitter—"What is my life? It went to be your shadow"—and Seti is exhausted—"There is no more life to be demanded of me / Than I've already given" (1:137). Moses recognizes defeat and is momentarily stunned by the loss in which he and his cause are implicated:

> The shadows are too many.
> All was right, except this, all, the reason,
> The purpose, the justice, except this culmination.
> Good has turned against itself and become
> Its own enemy. Have we to say that truth
> Is only punishment? What must we say
> To be free of the bewildering mesh of God?
> Where is my hand to go to? Rameses,
> There's no more of me than this. This is all:
> I followed a light into a blindness.
>
> (1:138)

This is the crisis point of the play: guilt or at least responsibility for destruction has been turned against Moses and against his God more pointedly than before. Anath presses upon him the eternal unfairness of life's indifference to death:

> Rameses has died,
> And the air stands ready in the wilderness to take you in.
> Rameses has died. Tomorrow the lizards
> Will be sparkling on the rocks. Why aren't you dancing
> With such liberty for such starving souls?
>
> (1:140)

How is Moses to deal with the price exacted for God's purpose: "Why was it I that had to be disaster to you? / I do not know why the necessity of God / Should feed on grief; but it seems so" (1:140). This is the point at which Fry later considered he should have offered a fuller discussion. Moses swiftly considers three alternatives. First is a life of guilt—"The blame could impale me / For ever"—in the form of personal despair—"I could be so sick of heart / That who asked for my life should have it." Second is cynical acceptance: "or I could see / Man's life go forward only by guilt and guilt. / Then we should always be watching Rameses die." His third alternative is an assertion of continuing existence: Rameses "is here pursuing the ends of the world" (1:140). This conclusion, Fry later commented, was too sudden, brief, and enigmatic to offer a positive counterpoise to Moses' despair. Because this is an Old Testament story, Fry cannot make use of New Testament terminology to direct the audience's understanding, and the way in which Rameses is not dead but has laid aside his mortality is left unexplained and unrealized.

On the level of theme and imagery, the appeal to immortality is massively outweighed by the rest of the play. The Exodus, the "going out," of the central myth is a release from three hundred years of bondage for the Israelites, but we do not see their departure; we have seen only the lengthy, punishing power game between God and Pharaoh, extended by a brutality that is not peculiar to Pharaoh or the Egyptians, but, it is suggested by the case of Shendi, is endemic to human nature. Because the positive aspects of the play are not only delayed and brief but also outweighed by a flood of death imagery, there is difficulty in presenting the idea of a just and benevolent God.

Moses is the character around whom death gathers; his touch kills more than it liberates during the action. He claims to be the ghost of his former adopted Egyptian self—"The prince of Egypt died the day he fled" (1:66), marked by the killing of the overseer: "I killed an Egyptian / And buried him in the sand. Does one deed then / Become our immortal shape?" (1:128). His former self is dead: "And he killed / His Egyptian self in the self of that Egyptian / And buried that self in the sand" (1:60). And in spite of Seti's claims that the murder itself has died—"his deed died. Ten years long / He has lugged this dead thing after him" (1:61)—when Moses appears, it is in "so ghostly a homecoming" that it is in vain for Seti to urge, "Isn't it time we laid the crippling ghost that haunts us?" (1:66). Rameses sees him "as absolute as man's death" (1:86). But the imagery of the other characters too insists on the atmosphere of mortality. We first meet Rameses on his return from hunting birds on the marshes. Sensitive, he has been strangely affected by the death of one bird, and death and darkness are associated in the image as so often in the plays:

> I watched his nerves flinching
> As they felt how dark that darkness was.
> I found myself trying to peer into his death.
> It seemed a long way down. The morning and it
> Were oddly separate,
> Though the bird lay in the sun: separate somehow
> Even from contemplation.
>   (1:64)

This may seem a peripheral passage designed to develop characterization of Rameses, but it is more than that; it is a pointer to a major theme of the play. Death is a mystery, not to be reasoned about or contemplated on the same terms as life, and if we see death, even that of a bird, as always a momentous transition into mystery, then the deliberate piling of death on death becomes intolerable. The image of the dead bird is related to the human deaths in Miriam's recollection of persecutions: "We have a wildfowl quality of blood, / Moses, temptation for sportsmen" (1:76).

Victim and predator are part of this web of imagery of death and point to the central problem: why does God permit destruction, suffering, evil? Like Blake questioning the forges and creator of the tyger, Moses asks:

> What spirit made the hawk? a bird obedient
> To grace, a bright lash on the cheek of the wind
> And drawn and ringed with feathered earth and sun,
> An achievement of eternity's birdsmith. But did he
> Also bleak the glittering charcoal of the eyes
> And sharpen beak and claws on his hone of lust?
>
> (1:81)

To the baffled human being, this uniting of beauty and destruction is inexplicable; he concludes, "A quarrel in God's nature" (1:81). Even the labors of the Israelites are directed not to building a treasure house as Exodus has it but to the construction of the pyramid, an image immediately familiar to the audience and most significant in its function as a tomb.

Moses is a powerful character, but the brooding intensity of his presence manifests itself in obscure language. To Seti's first questions about his return, Moses replies:

> To be close to this that up to now
> Has been a pain in the mind, not yet
> Possessing the mind, but so increasing
> It has driven me here, to be in myself the pain,
> To be the pain's own life.
>
> (1:67)

Here are the elements of repetition, participles and accumulative circling toward meaning, that appeared as signs of T. S. Eliot's influence in *The Boy with a Cart,* and these periphrases and spiritual implications make understanding difficult for Moses' interlocutors within the play, as well as for the

audience. Evidently Moses has returned to Egypt to effect the physical release
of his people, but he also is aware of the need to promote their spiritual regen-
eration, to justify their right to life, and to understand his own place and
God's place in the process. Therefore Aaron's practical "You will find the approach / And the means you want, I'm confident. Something / Will soon
open a way to action" (1:77) is a reply to words that show more than hesita-
tion about strategy:

> But still I need to know how good
> Can be strong enough to break out of the possessing
> Arms of evil. I am there, beyond myself,
> If I could reach to where I am.
>
> (1:77)

Naturally Aaron is puzzled by Moses' universal and eternal perspective, expressed through terms of spiritual experience: "our need is something different: / To confront ourselves, to create within ourselves / Existence which
cannot fail to be fulfilled" (1:85). He heralds the final visitation of the destroying angel thus:

>   The sound
> Of God. It comes; after all, it comes. It made
> The crucial interchange of earth with everlasting;
> Found and parted the stone lips of this
> Egyptian twilight in the speech of souls,
> Moulding the air of all the world, and desiring
> Into that shell of shadow, a man's mind—
> Into my own.
>
> (1:126)

Aaron, bewildered, can only ask, "What was told? What was said?" (1:126).
He understandably says of Moses that "he is in a space somewhere between /
The human and inhuman" (1:129). Unlike though the plays are in other
respects, The Firstborn creates similar problems of interpretation for the audience as does Eliot's The Family Reunion in that actions and behavior have a
significance in metaphysical as well as physical terms, and the character given
the function of suggesting this very complex significance tends to suffer from
an excess of abstract speeches, which neither mesh with the material frame of
reference of the other characters nor are extensive enough for the audience to
grasp the concepts as the action presses on.

Apart from the sheer difficulty of presenting meaning through these enigmatic speeches, Moses' characterization also suffers from a style that is frequently epigrammatic. The play is full of vivid imagery—just as much as Fry's middle comedies, if not more so—but Moses has more of the self-contained unexpected images that do not grow out of the context and mood: "The golden bear Success," he says, "Hugs a man close to its heart; and breaks his bones" (1:104); "The plainest soldier is sworn to the service of riddles" (1:100); and "Our strategy is written on strange eternal paper" (1:100). Because he often corrects the ideas of others with his references to a higher level of meaning or with aphoristic appeals to eternal truths, Moses remains an authoritative and perhaps tormented but not lovable character.

The other characters also have a share of surprising epigrams. Aaron's way of claiming that the evening calm is ominous is to say, "The evening's a perjury! / Let none of us be duped by it" (1:98). Anath strangely compares her helplessness to that of "a fishwife who has been made to breed against / Her will" (1:108) and relates clumsy humanity to "drunk men with a key in the dark who stand / At the right door but cannot get out of the cold" (1:115). Rameses compares his precious childhood memories of Moses with the present when "the memory / Broke its wrappings, and stood speaking like a man / On a noonday terrace" (1:77). This is the sort of detached imagery that Denis Donoghue condemned as being Fry's, not his characters'.[2] But apart from a few such excursions, the voice of each character is individualized. Although both Anath and Miriam are embittered middle-aged women, given to ironic commentary on their lot, Miriam speaks in short units and assertive statements that suggest a suppressed violence in spite of her alleged cynicism:

> To you Shendi is always blameable.
> Because at last he can have ambitions,
> Because he's ripping up the bare boards
> His boyhood lay on, to make himself a fire
> Which will warm his manhood, we turn on him—yes,
> I also, as much as you—I stormed so.
>
> (1:122)

Anath, on the other hand, is given to understatement; she refers to the colossal tomb deprecatingly: "I could as happily lie / And wait for eternal life in something smaller" (1:56). Both Rameses and Seti ask questions persistently throughout their dialogue. Those of Rameses are requests for information or permission and express his insecure position, poised between boyhood and manhood, confused by life. Seti's questions are mainly rhetorical, instruments of domination and self-justification, appeals to a standard of material reasonableness. One of his favorite words is *will*, both in the sense of volition (his willpower) and of future time, a future he predicts and is determined to control.

Fry's writing here is again experimental. It is not the presence or frequency of images but their closeness or distance from what is being described that detracts from some speeches. We can accept the violence of "an inward knife scraped his eyes clean" (1:59) for sudden painful insight, but other images suggest no attributes that we can relate to their objects. Moses says that the sound of God "found and parted the stone lips of this Egyptian twilight in the speech of souls" (1:126), but the effort required to sort the implied parallels here is demanding of the audience. Why does the twilight have stone lips? Is it being likened to a huge statue, and why? Is the twilight literal or metaphorical? Fry explains that he intended the statue to express the effect of something hard and unyielding being forced to obey God. Half an hour in a literary seminar might result in an acceptable guide, but in the theater at least a general grasp has to be available quickly. Most of the play's images do, as they should, illuminate an unexpected aspect of their subject, but some have detached themselves too far for the spark of understanding to travel from one to the other. This particular problem of poetic drama—the stage at which the poetic expression of an idea becomes the difficult expression of an idea, too difficult to be seized on the wing by the audience—recurs even in the comedies, but Fry did not again overload one character with spiritual concepts in enigmatic verse.

Thor, with Angels

Thor, with Angels is a slighter work than *The Firstborn*. It was written for a religious festival and is performed less often than *The Boy with a Cart* or *A Sleep of Prisoners*, Fry's other festival pieces. Its poise between comedy and tragedy is uncertain, and this is significant because it shows Fry reworking the unresolved tragic theme of *The Firstborn* and moving toward reconciliation of destruction with meaningfulness, though perhaps not yet with total success. It was commissioned for the Canterbury Festival of 1948, and Fry takes as his subject the early history of Canterbury, at the point in A.D. 596 when St. Augustine arrives from Rome to reconvert Britain to Christianity. The play shows how this affects a pagan Jutish household in Kent. This is to be a reconversion because Britain had already been converted to Christianity under the later Roman occupation some centuries before, but Romans and Britons had been pushed out by the movements of Germanic invaders, and the present Jutish inhabitants and their rival settlers, the Saxons, worship the Germanic pantheon of gods.

The tragic victim in the play is Hoel, one of the last remaining Britons, still vaguely mindful of his baptism in the name of the One God. The Jutes have captured him in a battle against the Saxons, by whom the orphaned Hoel has been brought up in partial servitude. As in *The Firstborn* and *The Boy with a Cart*, the hand of God is revealed in a series of firm interventions. As the play opens, the Jutes are returning from battle in dismay and fear because a strange force has made Cymen, the head of the household, defend the young British captive against his own men:

> Like a madman, he saved this Briton when we'd have killed him:
> Burst in among us, blaspheming against Woden,
> Broke his sword in the air—he swore it broke
> Against a staggering light.
>
> (2:60)

Cymen's two sons and his two brothers-in-law are adamant that Hoel must be sacrificed at once, but Cymen cautiously demands time to find out the reason for the supernatural effect, in case it recurs. As Cymen rallies his family to libation to the gods Woden and Thor, his voice forms the words of the Christian admonition, "Let us love one another" (2:70), instead of the pagan toast. Provoked, he attacks Hoel after all but finds himself striking at his own son Quichelm and says in confusion: "It seems / All one, it seems all one. There's no distinction. / Which is my son?" (2:71).

Again like *The Firstborn* but unlike *The Boy with a Cart*, the divine purpose is concerned more with national spiritual development, not individual survival. These signs ultimately predispose Cymen and the Jutes to accept Augustine's message when summoned to the king's general assembly, but Hoel himself is killed by the warriors before their conversion is achieved. This time, however, death is not a tragic waste, unnecessary though it is. Its wider purpose in the play is to reflect the sacrifice of the crucifixion. Hoel is tied to a tree, as on a crucifix, to be speared by the Jutes, who ironically say this is "Woden's way, a Woden death" (2:106). More immediately, Cymen is able to demonstrate forgiveness instead of revenge as a means of establishing his own true conversion and of impressing its nature on his family. Finally, Hoel has been able to say, "Death, be to me like a hand that shades / My eyes, helping me to see / Into the light" (2:106). The death of Hoel signifies acceptance of God's will and hope of life after death. Yet there is always a feeling of tragic loss with the death of a young character like Hoel or Rameses, especially when it is not willed by the character. Hoel's repeated "Let me live, do, do, / Let me live" (2:106) is likely to stay in the audience's memory more than his final acquiescence.

The framework of values, nevertheless, is securely presented. Thor and the other gods are the purveyors of misery and unease, while the angels of Christianity bring confidence and a sense of mental contentment. The Norse gods are worshipped in an atmosphere of subservience and cringing foreboding; a permanent expectation of undeserved punishment hangs over even the more peaceful intervals. The pagans can never have a sense of being at home in their world; they exist from day to day on sufferance. Here Fry's world picture reasserts itself after its eclipse in *The Firstborn*. Much of the expression of the Jutes' placatory life-style is comic, as when Martina greets her brothers, "I knew you'd come today. / The cows this morning were all facing north" (2:58), and Cymen's wife protests, "Defeated? Have you come back defeated / When I sacrificed a good half goat?" and Cymen rejoins, "No doubt / The wrong half, my jewel" (2:62), but underneath is a sense of exclusion from the desired security. Cymen's indictment of the gods two-thirds of the way through the play has been implicit all along:

> The deed of death is done and done and always
> To do, death and death and death; and still
> We cannot come and stand between your knees.
> Why? By what stroke was the human flesh
> Hacked so separate from the body of life
> Beyond us? You make us to be the eternal alien
> In our own world.
>
> (2:94)

Human beings feel that they exist on sufferance only, and all misfortunes are taken personally. This illusion is eventually challenged when Cymen defiantly destroys the altar, crying, "Answer, then, answer . . . Come down and silence me!" (2:94), but the expectant silence is broken by the call of the king's man, with his message from the Christian missionaries: the words of Augustine are to provide an answer in full, and the "eternal alien" is to become "welcome to creation":

> The fearful silence
> Became the silence of great sympathy,
> The quiet of God and man in the mutual word.
> And never again need we sacrifice, on and on

And on, greedy of the gods' goodwill
But always uncertain.

(2:108)

Cymen's exposition of the new religion he is requiring his family to follow
is comparatively brief, but it stresses three times the claim that Christianity
makes "our lonely flesh / Welcome to creation" (2:108). Once fear of the
unpredictable gods is forgotten, the burden of fear can be laid upon the One
God: "God give us courage to exist in God" (2:110).

It is Merlin, a somewhat peripheral chorus figure calling himself "more
than half a pagan" (2:102) who gives a fuller explanation of the difference
between fear and trust. He celebrates the beauty of the natural world as a
pagan who "cannot drag his lips / Away from the breast of the earth, even to
grow / Into the maturity of heaven" (2:84), but beyond this he acknowl-
edges "the very obdurate pressure / Edging men towards a shape beyond /
The shape they know" (2:102). His practice is pagan, his knowledge is Christian, and though unnecessary to the plot of this play, Merlin is in fact one of
the most helpful characters in all of Fry's plays in his expression of a recurring
theme fundamental to the playwright's vision. Merlin is speaking for Fry in
expressing his view of spiritualization through the natural world. What
seems partly Merlin's aged, sagelike fatalism is not merely this but suggests
the perspective of the Christian who need not waste anguish on earthly vicis-
situdes once he has come to share a trust in God's purposes:

Who, apart
From ourselves, can see any difference between
Our victories and our defeats, dear sir?
Not beast, nor bird, nor even the anticipating
Vulture watching for the battle's end,
Nor a single mile of devoted dispassionate ground.
All indifferent . . .
. . . Quest and conquest and quest again. It might well
Make you fretful if you weren't expecting it.

(2:83)

Merlin is answering part of Cymen's dissatisfaction and finds a place even for
death in his long final speech. Here he puts forward Fry's interest in the pattern of nature, imagined as laid down in a blueprint in "the slumbering rock,"
so that the more transient and beautiful aspects of nature are regularly em-

bodied as "all dreams out of the slumbering rock" (2:101). Everything in the
world is guided by an underlying shape, a kind of Platonic template:

> Each dream answering to a shape
> Which was in dream before the shapes were shapen
> Each growing obediently to a form,
> To its own sound, shrill or deep, to a life
> In water or air, in light or night or mould;
> By sense or thread perceiving,
> Eye, tendril, nostril, ear; to the shape of the dream
> In the ancient slumbering rock.
>
>   (2:101)

This passage continues to relate death, as well as all these manifestations of
life, to the will of God:

> And above the shapes of life, the shape
> Of death, the singular shape of the dream dissolving,
> Into which all obediently come.
> And above the shape of death, the shape of the will
> Of the slumbering rock, the end of the throes of sleep
> Where the stream of the dream wakes in the open eyes
> Of the sea of the love of the morning of the God.
>
>   (2:102)

Merlin's choral function is his main function, and his legendary identity as
magician and prophet gives authority to his pronouncements, as his indifference to Thor and Woden helps undermine their hold on the Jutes, but as a
chorus he is less naturally part of the setting than the People of the South of
England in *The Boy with a Cart*. Structurally, however, another important
function is that his interventions lower the tension and give variety of tempo
to the growing conflict between Cymen and his family. There are three increasing peaks of excitement in the play, the first when Cymen's account of
his battlefield possession is followed by onstage miraculous control of his actions and words. The second is the offstage wolf attack leading to a further
onstage clash of wills between Cymen and his more murderous tribesmen,
and the last is the brutal and noisy killing of Hoel while Cymen is away.

Between the first and second crises, Merlin is literally unearthed from
centuries-long hibernation in a quarry, and his amiable detachment extends
the peaceful conversation among the women, servants, and Hoel. After the
second climax, Merlin's long lyrical speech reestablishes hope of a happy

ending, but it is a deceptive hope. Martina and Hoel's tentative love scene
that follows is not the symbol of reconciliation but the "grounds for getting
him where the gods want him" (2:104), a pretext for Hoel's murder by the
eavesdropping warriors. By this time, Merlin has wandered back to hibernation, and the struggle and screaming of Hoel's death scene subsides into
Cymen's lament and forgiveness. Revelation has come too late for Hoel, but
Cymen is able to focus on the significance of the new beliefs for the Jutes in a
more useful way than Merlin's placid long-term view. Merlin's paganism is a
limitation to his role as spokesman, a role that would be more happily integrated by a philosopher-saint if such had been available in this episode; but
the possible candidate for this role, Augustine, remains offstage. It is fitting,
however, that, as at the end of *Murder in the Cathedral*, the ordinary characters who are left to adjust their lives to the crisis and martyrdom have their
own last words, speaking for the ordinary, struggling human being and relat-
ing the meaning to the audience.

Fry's language here is still at the same stage as in *The Firstborn*, though
with some differences. As Merlin's speeches show, there are traces of the
thoughtful reiteration noted in *The Boy with a Cart*, but here they are spun
out into quite a different rhythm. Certainly there are echoes of the earlier
Eliotian style where the same subjects—the effort to define a complex metaphysical idea, the effects of cyclical repetition—are expressed by Merlin:

> . . . Still I observe the very obdurate pressure
> Edging men towards a shape beyond
> The shape they know. Now and then, by a spurt
> Of light, they manage the clumsy approximation,
> Overturn it, turn again, refashion
> Nearer the advising of their need.
>
> (2:102)

But the units of phrasing are shorter here and the hesitating movement
more limited. When Cymen describes the Jutes' ritual gestures toward the
unknown, he is using Eliotian imagery, but the format is a crisp series of
phrases building up to a firm climax:

> The blood flows, the ground soaks it up,
> The poisoned nightshade grows, the fears go on,
> The dread of doom gropes into the bowels,

> And hope, with her ambitious shovel, sweats
> To dig the pit which swallows us at last.
>
> (2:93)

Because most of the characters are Germanic, this play uses an appropriate stylistic feature in that their speech is characterized by heavy alliteration similar to that of Anglo-Saxon verse. Cymen's previously cited speech uses it sparingly and does not approach the three alliterations per line of conventional Anglo-Saxon poetry, but the effect is there, especially in the battle descriptions:

> Like a madman he saved this Briton when we would have killed him:
> Burst in amongst us, blaspheming against Woden.
> Broke his sword in the air—he swore it broke
> Against a staggering light—and stood roaring,
> Swaying in a sweat of wax.
>
> (2:60)

This is formal and formulaic, but Cymen's alliterative repetitions—"The deed of death is done and done, and always / To do, death and death and death" (2:94)—are not Anglo-Saxon or archaic but simply forceful, and his sense of alienation from the universe of hostile or indifferent gods is not Eliotian; it is reminiscent less of Thomas Becket than of Samuel Beckett:

> Under me, silence; round me, silence, air,
> The wind hushing the world to hear
> The wind hushing the world; and over me,
> Silence upon silence upon silence.
> Unuttering vapour, unutterable void.
>
> (2:91)

Cymen's anguish is individual as well as representative of all his fellow Jutes' experience, and here it is not formulaic in style; it finds its own rhythm, and the alliteration is noticeable but not regular.

The shorter dialogue is sometimes less successful in its expression of personality and feeling. Expression tends to be too elaborate for functional dialogue, as when Cymen expands on his incidental inability to sleep—"An occasional shadow across my bed from a cloud / Of weariness, but the glare of the brain persisted" (2:80)—or Osmer summons his brothers: "I've got a screw of courage you can chew" (2:99).

Fry was praised for his "Elizabethan" style or condemned for his overindulgence in decoration in his better known comedies, but in *Thor,* the elaboration has a delaying effect on the dialogue without the enlivening effect of the other more consistently witty plays. Kenneth Pickering suggests that in *Thor,* "the more interesting underlying ideas are secondary to dull theatrical qualities."[3] In general this sort of conclusion can only be subjective and can be overturned by an imaginative production at any time, but one could provisionally say that a director would have to work hard against the retarding qualities of some of the dialogue. On the other hand, the underlying ideas are founded in the action and are interpreted fully in the longer speeches, which depend heavily on the main actors. Both action and long speeches clearly insist on the place of human beings in the natural world, as well as representing death as an acceptance of God rather than an unwilled punishment by God. These ideas are more fully developed later, but their significance here shows Fry overcoming the unreconciled pessimism of *The Firstborn.*

Chapter Four

Hints of Hidden Messages:
A *Phoenix Too Frequent*

A Phoenix Too Frequent was written for E. Martin Browne's season of poetic drama at the Mercury Theatre in 1946. Fry's play stands out from the other participants, which included Ronald Duncan's *This Way to the Tomb* and Anne Ridler's *The Shadow Factory,* in its thoroughly comic tone. All of the plays of that season have themes that ultimately are positive. Duncan's play, for instance, uses satire and caricature but is predominantly corrective. In the masque (or first) half, it follows in detail the spiritual struggle and temptations of St. Anthony, and in the antimasque (or second) half, it integrates a mocking survey of modern society with the recognition of the continuing human need to cope with bereavement, disaster, and loneliness, played against the background of the saint's tomb. Fry's play, however, is not only positive but positively ebullient. Although *Phoenix* takes place entirely within a tomb, the dead body of its new occupant lying covered upstage throughout, the vitality and energy of life dispel the potential gloom of this situation.

It was evident in *The Firstborn* that divine purpose and tragic waste were incomprehensibly bound up together and that Fry's final insistence on God's purpose was at odds with the sense of tragic loss. In *Phoenix*, grief and loss are not intended to engage the audience's sympathies, though this again causes some dislocation at the end of the play. The heroine, Dynamene, is planning to die of sorrow and hunger in vigil beside her dead husband, and her maid, Doto, is, like the archetypal confidante of tragedy, going to share her mistress's fate. But Doto's opening soliloquy, which sets the tone of the play, leaves little doubt that suffering will be slight. Her sense of self-sacrifice is qualified:

> Honestly, I would rather have to sleep
> With a bald bee-keeper who was wearing his boots
> Than spend more days fasting and thirsting and crying

> In a tomb. I shouldn't have said that. Pretend
> I didn't hear myself.
>
> (2:7)

The audience at once notes the leveling effect of this alternative: death is reduced to a comic choice, and this is to be Fry's comic method throughout the play—the incongruous juxtapositions and comparisons not only produce humorous anticlimax but undermine the tragic attitudes as they are assumed.

So far Fry's view that "the poetry is the action and the action—apart even from the words—is the figure of the poetry" is borne out (*An Experience of Critics*, 27). The poetry of Dynamene's lamentations has been so full of vitality—"My husband, you have left a wake in my soul. / You cut the glassy water with a diamond keel" (2:8)—that her fading into silence is highly improbable. When the young soldier, Tegeus, who is guarding the bodies of six executed men hanging on trees outside the tomb, intrudes first his admiration and then his love on the lamenting widow, her capitulation to his adoration (aided by plentiful wine on a fasting stomach) is no surprise. Dynamene is dynamic and a character of creation, not annihilation. Possibly the next twist of the plot, whereby Tegeus finds that one of his bodies has been stolen while he has dallied in the tomb, thus leaving him due for court-martial and hanging in his turn, provides rather more of a serious threat. But again Tegeus's speeches, while rising to some heights of heroism, are undercut by incongruity before they end:

> For god's sake let me die
> On a wave of life, Dynamene, with an action
> I can take some pride in. How could I settle to death
> Knowing that you last saw me stripped and strangled
> On a holly tree? Demoted first then hanged!
>
> (2:46)

What is a surprise is Dynamene's solution to the crisis: she offers her husband's body as a substitute for the missing corpse. Her pragmatism—"he has no further use / For what he left of himself to lie with us here"(2:48)—is in such contrast with her earlier mourning that it focuses attention on the suddenness of her transformation, partly overlooked in the progress of the action. The audience is relieved at Tegeus's prospective escape but also shocked.

Apart from this, Fry's handling of his source material controls the audience's view of the events in the plot so that their reaction is sympathetic and approving. His note says, "The story was got from Jeremy Taylor who had it from Petronius." Jeremy Taylor is distantly disapproving; the nameless Ephesian woman's mourning is a "violent passion" that "layed all her spirits in wildness and dissolution," and her sudden love for the young soldier is equally unreasonable and unreliable.[1] The outline of events is the same, but Taylor's estimate of them is unhopeful. The classic virtues of moderation— "discipline, and the conduct of reason, and the proportions of temperate humanity"—are missing in both the widow's intemperate grief and her sudden consolation.[2] Thus the conclusion leaves the couple "to enjoy a love which might change as violently as her grief had done." Among other images, Taylor develops a comparison with "the wilde foragers of Lybia," wild beasts that are prompted by the sudden refreshment of springs in the desert to "strange marriages" in which the lioness and the panther mate to produce "a monster that men call unnatural."[3] The point here is that what for Taylor is uniformly unnatural and to be condemned is for Fry a thoroughly natural development—the natural force of life supervening over the first, unnatural phase of despair. Fry ends on a celebratory note that has none of Taylor's misgivings about future change.

The celebration at the end is one of several indications that the plot is not merely what it seems on the surface. The final sequence has Virilius, the dead husband, saving the soldier Tegeus by being substituted for the missing corpse and therefore for the guilty Tegeus. Tegeus's redemption reflects human redemption through the sacrifice of the risen Christ; the criminals hang on "five plane trees and a holly," the missing one being stolen from the holly tree, traditionally a symbol of Christ's cross. The women have suffered almost three days in the tomb (changed, as Stanley Wiersma points out, from Petronius's five days) so that Virilius, like Christ, restores life to the other characters on the third day.[4] Tegeus has been whimsically renamed by Dynamene as "Chromis. It has a bread-like sound" (2:28), and apart from the tenuous hint of baptism, this means that the final celebration—"There's some wine unfinished in this bowl. / I'll share it with you" (2:49)—unites the Christian Communion elements of bread and wine and has a eucharistic significance of gratitude, commemoration, and celebration. Wiersma traced Tegeus-Chromis's reference to "section six, paragraph three of the regulations" to the final verses that lie in the third division of chapter 6 of St. Paul's epistle to the Romans (Rom. 6:23): "The wages of sin is death; but the gift of God is eternal life through Jesus Christ our Lord." Fry has confirmed that he had been reading and discussing Paul's epistles as he wrote the play. All except the substitution of Virilius are unobstrusive enough that, although critics have since examined them in detail, the average audience would pass them by. Fry says: "I wrote the play out of my general state of mind at the time, without wishing for any precise definition: hoping that what truth was in it would come across to an audience who had no knowledge of Paul's writings or much interest in Christianity."[5]

Within the plot, the parallel is not to be stressed too much. The love of God and the burden of sin do not afflict these pagans, who have a mild concern for their "extremely / Complicated gods" but unlike the Jutes in *Thor* show no particular interest in serving or pleasing them. Here the philosophy of the play moves in concert with the comic genre and the audience's desire for a happy ending. Because this is a romantic comedy, the characters' views of the world are of a familiar romantic kind. Love must win over death (and the parallel between earthly and divine love is traditional in literature), and Tegeus and Dynamene feel that they were destined to fulfill this special and unique love. Tegeus-Chromis says:

> I was born entirely
> For this reason. I was born to fill a gap
> In the world's experience, which had never known
> Chromis loving Dynamene.
>
> > (2:34)

On one level, this is the typical egotism of all romantic lovers, but on another, it celebrates the amazing variety of the world, evident in the poetic descriptions, each element of that variety having its own worth. And the "reason" underlying this scheme of things is the will of God to which created things consciously or unconsciously conform, as Tegeus seems to realize:

> I followed my future here,
> As we all do if we're sufficiently inattentive
> And don't vex ourselves with questions; or do I mean
> Attentive? If so, attentive to what?
>
> > (2:27)

Unity with the beloved mirrors unity with God and is a secular way of making the lonely individual at home in the universe, as is later suggested in *Venus Observed*. Thus Tegeus and Dynamene are comic but sincere in their romantic badinage. It is important that their attraction is not the mere drunken sexuality of Petronius's and Taylor's story because they need to be seen as striving for a solution that combines the unselfishness as well as the selfishness of romantic love.

Searching for her destiny has led Dynamene to the wrong conclusion that she should die. Tegeus's alternative vision of their fates, however self-interested, offers a greater harmony with the world they both describe in such loving detail. Because unity and purpose do not come instinctively to human beings, they are at a disadvantage compared with, for example, the anony-mous population of insects which "freckle the light and go and come with-out / A name among them" (2:27). Virilius, Dynamene's late husband, had evidently solved the problems of living in the wrong way; instead of finding a place in the bountiful variety of the world, he has been the sort of person who tries to cut variety down to size. Amid Dynamene's regrets for the vital uni-verse lost to Virilius, her description of his "punctual eye," his "cautious voice which made / Balance-sheets sound like Homer and Homer sound / Like balance-sheets" (2:11) suggests that he did not feel the joys or conflicts of ex-istence: "To Virilius it was not so; his brain was an ironing-board / For all crumpled indecision" (2:24).

Tegeus-Chromis is also wrong when he praises Dynamene's self-sacrifice because it is so simple and perfect, grief carried to its logical conclusion with-out being qualified by thoughts of self or society: "To have found life, after all, unambiguous!" (2:18). Dynamene too is wrong to pursue this single self-willed way. Tegeus sees it as

> what is undeceiving and uncorrupt
> And undivided; this is the clear fashion
> For all souls, a ribbon to bind the unruly
> Curls of living.
>
> (2:18)

But the curls of living are too unruly to be subdued by willpower, as Dynamene soon finds.

In this comedy, death is presented in a different way from the wasteful forced sacrifices of *The Firstborn* and *Thor*. "Death is a kind of love. / Not anything I can explain" (2:14), says Tegeus, approving Dynamene's vigil. Fry himself in a lecture explained this further as having "one very human meaning. In the simplest terms love desires union, to be of one flesh with the beloved." Also, "If we don't love life and value it deeply our acceptance of death becomes meaningless, a shrug of the shoulders, instead of an ultimate act of life."[6] It may seem that Dynamene loves and values life at the begin-ning of the play, but this love is inoperative as long as she does not realize it. She evokes the beauty of the world, but does not fully register the implica-tions of renouncing it forever, in her single-minded lamentation for Virilius.

Like Thomas Mendip in a later play, Dynamene is inspired only by negative feelings, a rejection of the unaccommodating circumstances; it is a kind of shrug, not a kind of love. As Doto puts it, "Death's a new interest in life" (2:10), and neither woman has accepted that ultimate separation of life from death, perceived momentarily by Rameses as "a long way down . . . separate somehow / From contemplation" (1:64).

Dynamene's eloquent tribute to the world, now lost to Virilius, shows her own continuing ties to it. She is celebrating life, not bidding farewell to it in her set-piece speech:

> What a mad blacksmith creation is
> Who blows his furnaces until the stars fly upward
> And iron Time is hot and politicians glow
> And bulbs and roots sizzle into hyacinth
> And orchis, and the sand puts out the lion,
> Roaring yellow, and the oceans bud with porpoises,
> Blenny, tunny and the almost unexisting
> Blindfish; throats are cut, the masterpiece
> Looms out of labour; nations and rebellions
> Are spat out to hang on the wind.
>
> (2:12)

This may be all "gone / In one Virilius, wearing his office tunic" (2:12), but it is evidently still present for Dynamene. "Where is animation now?" she concludes, but she has just shown animation everywhere in her speech. The life force that makes the ocean bud porpoises is present in herself and is soon to undermine her sorrow, as she recognizes in the growth images of leaf and fronds put out by "the separate meaningless will" of the "inveterate body" (2:23). Dynamene's appreciation of the external world extends in fact from the mainly natural elements to include every variety of surroundings:

> Even the metal and plume of the rose garden,
> And the forest where the sea fumes overhead
> In vegetable tides, and particularly
> The entrance to the warm baths in Arcite Street
> Where we first met.
>
> (2:11)

The tomb itself is dark and grim, but Dynamene is creating these pictures of the world outside from the fund of vitality within her. Tegeus-Chromis, equally full of vitality, contributes images of his birthplace, Pyxa, with its beechwoods, white owls, doves, cresses, and kingcups. Doto's contribution is the less romantic, more earthy, and heterogenous memories of her highly individual lovers and her uncle's hardware shop in the country: "Basins, pots, ewers and alabaster birds" (2:9). One of Doto's functions is to express through her sexual preoccupations the persistence of the "separate meaning-less will" that is perhaps meaningless only to the individual but has a purpose for humanity as a whole. She thinks of experience, grief, and memory all in terms of men, so that her motive for investigating the existence of souls in Hades is that "I like to know / What I'm getting with a man" (2:14). A lit-tle of Tegeus's wine has her unavailingly and unheard pestering the reverent soldier with "Do you love me, handsome?" (2:18) Her comic insufficiency to the tragic role is an example of the powers of instinct and confusion; her be-havior prepares for Dynamene's attraction to the vital Tegeus-Chromis.

Fry has built up the appeal of life in its variety of experience, in the beauty and absurdity of people and objects, to ratify Dynamene's change of heart. As far as her attraction to Tegeus-Chromis is concerned, this is amusing but understandable. Her offer of Virilius's body to an ignominious if necessary fate, however, is harder to accept and suggests a callousness and egotism im-plied in Petronius and Taylor but that Fry has tried to eliminate from his sym-pathetic portrait. Although Dynamene argues "I loved / His life not his death" (2:49), she has, after all, been fasting beside the body, which implies some significance attached to the physical remains. The problem is to make Dynamene's position—continuing affection for the memory of Virilius but indifference to his body—acceptable in its unconventionality. As in *The Firstborn*, this complex process is presented late in the play, in the last few minutes of the action, and it is not developed fully enough to carry the au-dience's considered assent. Instead the speed of delivery means that the play falls back on comic convention; it is a solution to a problem, without needing to have all the implications, responsibilities, and emotional ramifications weighed in the balance. Nor do we have to see the practical fulfillment of Dynamene's suggestion, when the body of Virilius is carried out and strung up, a gruesome necessity that might cast some doubt on her idealized, "He moves again in the world, accomplishing our welfare" (2:49).

One critical reaction to *Phoenix* was that it had "no plot," an accusation leveled at many and various other modern dramatists from Shaw to Arnold Wesker. By this, critics of the forties and fifties seemed to mean that there was no puzzle and denouement, no mystery. *Theatre World* claimed that the play had "many stage virtues but not shape," and, surprisingly, "it is too long. Pruning of the poet's words would add to its point".[7] Dynamene's move from one state to its opposite, however, gives a strong plot line, and Tegeus-

Chromis's similar but more rapid move from admiration to subversion of her grief is a secondary and complementary line.

The direction of the plot is, roughly, from depression to triumph. Even the expository opening, in which Doto's soliloquy and conversation with Dynamene explain the situation and background, is not unrelieved in its gloom, and Tegeus's entry and innocent weakening of Doto's willpower with his wine suggest a possible change of action. Dynamene's indignation at his intrusion is a first but minor contrary movement to the optimistic progress, and again the comic digressions minimize this setback. Once Doto has sunk to sleep in her turn, the longest sequence in the play is devoted to Dynamene's gradually growing interest in Tegeus and discovery of topics of conversation, mainly their mutual admiration for each other's physical appearance but also appreciation of wine and the countryside about Pyxa, an obvious revival of Dynamene's involvement with the world that Virilius has left. Moments of remorse punctuate this progression, but by the time Tegeus remembers that he is supposed to be on duty, both are quite determined to enjoy their new fortune to the full.

Doto's awakening not only fills the interval of Tegeus's excursion but underlines the comic reversal of Dynamene's attitude by her untimely recapitulation of the arguments for death; this broader comedy, increased by Dynamene's efforts to get rid of an embarrassing witness, then contrasts abruptly with the plunge into dismay when Tegeus returns with the news of his loss, prospective execution, and determination on suicide. This is given some emphasis and wavers between lightness and threatening tragedy, though the anticlimaxes suggest that it is not a serious threat—"How can they hang you for losing a dead man? / They must have wanted to lose him, or they wouldn't / Have hanged him" (2:46)—as do the neat epigrams:

> DYNAMENE: Chromis
> You must never die, never! It would be
> An offence against truth.
>
> TEGEUS: I cannot live to be hanged.
> It would be an offence against life.
>
> (2:47)

Nonetheless there is more pathos and fear in Tegeus's determination than in Dynamene's earlier mourning—"For god's sake let me die / On a wave of life, Dynamene, with an action / I can take some pride in" (2:46)—even if he lapses into hurt pride at how he would look—"Demoted first and then hanged." Enough time is spent on Tegeus's explanations and desperation to

convince Dynamene that the problem is serious and the audience that there is
a slight possibility of things going wrong. Having postponed the happy ending, Fry has to settle the conclusion one way or another. Structurally, a long
discussion thrashing out the moral and emotional implications of using
Virilius's body would cause an unhappy sagging in the tension of the action
just when it has been wound up doubly high, however needful such a discussion seems from the point of view of content. Dynamene's scruples thus fall
casualty to the rhythm of the action.

The structural reversal of Dynamene's mourning pose and of Tegeus's initial reverence for it is a basically comic process. The humor of the play as a
whole reflects this fundamental comic inconsistency, whereby we are contin-
ually confronted with pleasantly unexpected incongruities in both words and
action. Doto's pose of tragic contempt for Tegeus's first offer of food is comically reversed by her double take at the sight of his supper: "I'll turn my back
on you. It means utter / Contempt. Eat? Utter contempt. Oh, little new
rolls! (2:15)." Obviously the reader as well as the audience can see that her
turning her back is followed by a backward glance at the food and a total
change of expression and gesture; then this weakening is thwarted after all by
Tegeus's response to her words: he whisks the rolls away from her relenting
grasp, saying, "Forget it, forget it; please forget it" (2:15). Similarly Tegeus
wilts under Dynamene's wrathful condemnation of his intrusion and starts to
leave, only to be stopped by Doto:

> Hey, I don't think so, I shouldn't say so. Come
> Down again, uniform. Do you think you're going
> To half kill an unprotected lady and then
> Back out upwards?
>
> (2:21)

Tegeus's fluctuating feelings have literally and visibly carried him halfway up
the steps out of the tomb before Dynamene's attractions—"How can I?
Beauty's bit is between my teeth" (2:21)—bring him back to her in a comic
enactment of the different directions his mind is taking. But much of the
humor is verbal and depends on the properties of language itself rather than
or as well as contradictions of thought.

In spite of the connotations of fire and air of the title, *Phoenix* is pervaded
by imagery of sea and vegetation, though light and stars increasingly dominate as the action proceeds. Dynamene wakes first from a dream of Virilius as
a ship—"The figurehead / Bore his own features, so serene in the brow /
And hung with a little seaweed" (2:8)—and her memories of "the forest

where the sea fumes overhead / In vegetable tides" (2:11) are developed in the prolonged description of the scene decorating Tegeus's drinking bowl, a decoration he has designed. This depicts the god Bacchus, abducted by pirates, on a ship that has miraculously begun to sprout vines and leaves:

> The corded god, tied also by the rays
> Of the sun, and the astonished ship erupting
> Into vines and vine-leaves, inverted pyramids
> Of grapes, the uplifted hands of the men (the raiders)
> And here the headlong sea, itself almost
> Venturing into leaves and tendrils.
>
> (2:23)

This unity of sea and vegetation leads to Dynamene's comment shortly afterward that the inveterate body "insists on leaf, / Puts out, with a separate meaningless will, / Fronds to intercept the thankless sun" (2:24). The secular impact of the vegetation myth of recurring rebirth—associated with both Bacchus and Christ—is working its way out through Dynamene and Tegeus too, and the driving force of life is symbolized by proliferating vegetation. Dynamene then returns to the coercive and destructive power of the ocean for a less reassuring image: "When the thoughts would die, the instincts will set sail / For life. And when the thoughts are alert for life / The instincts will rage to be destroyed on the rocks" (2:24). Tegeus particularly begins to associate Dynamene with light, both briefly—"I'm looking directly into your light" (2:29)—and more extensively. Other women, he says, were "never you":

> never you . . . not more
> Than reflectively, stars lost and uncertain
> In the sea, compared with the shining salt, the shiners,
> The galaxies, the clusters, the bright grain whirling
> Over the black threshing-floor of space.
>
> (2:35)

The conventional imagery of light for beauty then blends with the conflict of light and life with darkness and death at the end, when Tegeus is steeling himself: "To do the impossible, to go from the light / That keeps you . . . O dark, it does" (2:48). There is a confirmation of the message that Dynamene has a destiny set out for her that she was wrongly seeking to change:

                                              I was wrong
                  To want you to keep our vows existent
                  In the vacuum that's coming. It would make you
                  A heaviness to the world, when you should be,
                  As you are a form of light.

                                              (2:48)

One subtle but distinct shift of practice in *Phoenix* may relate to its comic
genre. As in *The Boy with a Cart* but unlike *The Firstborn* and *Thor*, information is always given forcibly but simply, though this may include brief imagery of a surprising but easily related kind, such as, "It's morning; I see a
thin dust of daylight / Blowing on to the steps" (2:29). More lengthy or obscure metaphors are formally presented, not assumed to be part of straightforward conversation. They are elevated above the register of the rest of the
verse by a comic seeking after effect, a consciously assumed formality, or the
inspired hyperbole of the lover. Thus Doto says that "I feel sung, madam, by
a baritone / In mixed company with everyone pleased" (2:10). The initial
comparison of (roughly) "I am like a song" is subjected to comic elaboration,
its increasing detail mischievously carrying it further and further away from
its origins. Tegeus and Dynamene are both formally living up to their assumed roles. In Tegeus's speech of farewell, signaled by the formulaic "it only
remains for me to thank you," he returns to music imagery to say that he will
remember Dynamene "for however long I may be played by this poor musi-
cian, existence" (2:24). Dynamene is obviously presenting her self-image as
she wishes it to be seen, its grandiose melancholy characterizing her vanity as
well as adding humor, when she threatens what would happen "if I were still
of the world, and not cloistered / In a colourless landscape of winter
thought, / Where the approaching Spring is desired oblivion" (2:20).
    Lovers conventionally express themselves in hyperbole to convey their ex-
cessive feelings and new vision of the world. Dynamene tells Tegeus that he
"falls easily into superlatives," evidenced by his pleading for a kiss:

                              Oh, when I cross
                  Like this the hurt of the little space between us
                  I come a journey from the wrenching ice
                  To walk in the sun.

                                              (2:36)

She too is hyperbolic, if not superlative, in praising him:

> I can't look away from you. You use
> The lamplight and the moon so skilfully,
> So arrestingly, in and around your furrows.
> A humourous ploughman goes whistling to a team
> Of sad sorrow, to and fro in your brow
> And over your arable cheek.
>
> (2:35)

Here the elaborations of the imagery are not a baffling pursuit of complex meaning, as in *The Firstborn*—and the repetitive Eliotian rhythms have gone too—but betray tellingly the characters' attitudes and self-deceptions. In *Phoenix* Fry economically brings ridiculously inconsistent behavior and extravagant language together so that the audience constructs from these elements the comic effect of incongruity—of what the characters say and what they do—and pleasant surprise. This was to be a staple of Fry's comic method: the characters give their own points of view with a dazzling effect that is momentarily convincing, and at the same time the audience applies the more conventional or normal standards to what is said or done and laughs at the perceived incongruity.

Chapter Five

Condoning Creation in *The Lady's Not for Burning*

The Lady's Not for Burning was written in 1947 and produced in March 1948. In 1946 Fry had been writer-in-residence at the Arts Theatre, his duties mainly being to write a play. He had not succeeded during that time, but when the awaited play was completed, it was the property of the Arts. This has been one of Fry's most popular plays in Great Britain and all over the rest of the world, but on its first appearance, critics, as with *Phoenix*, were more exigent than audiences, specifically in again desiring more plot. The *Daily Telegraph* critic remarked, "The plot is a utility peg for verbiage . . . the thesis is merely that love will find a way"[1]; the *Times* critic said even more absolutely, "What will not be found there is a plot"[2]; and T. C. Worsley in the *New Statesman and Nation* recommended that Fry's "dazzling verbal invention . . . talent for devising situations and for creating character" must depend on "finding better fables. . . . For this is noticeably weak."[3]

Yet the plot now seems clear and is basically similar to that of *Phoenix*, in that one character has to persuade another that life is worth living. The play is set in "1400 either more or less or exactly," and here Thomas Mendip, a former soldier in his late twenties, arrives at the house of Hebble Tyson, the mayor of the small town of Cool Clary, demanding to be hanged. The world disgusts him, and he justifies his demand for an assisted passage out of it by claiming to have killed Old Skipps, the local rag and bone man, plus, as an afterthought, an anonymous pig man. A little later, the young and beautiful Jennet Jourdemayne seeks sanctuary from a pursuing mob of witch-hunters. The foundation stone of her accusation is that she has turned the same Old Skipps into a dog. In *Phoenix* it was the young soldier who praised life and the young woman who was determined to die; here the ex-soldier wishes to die, but his attitude is undermined by the young woman's beauty, pathetic fear of death, and eventual love for him. Expanding the story of Thomas and Jennet are the antics of Hebble Tyson's household, where the mayor's two nephews, Humphrey and Nicholas, and his clerk, Richard, all fall in love with

Humphrey's fiancée, Alizon, though Humphrey and Nicholas later abruptly transfer their affections to Jennet.

The structure of the play depends heavily on the management of the eleven characters, a cast perhaps larger than a commercial play would risk in the later twentieth century. The *Times* critic of 1949 compared the revived and transferred production with the text and noted the theatrical qualities supplied by the author for the director and company: "The text itself is found to provide every member of a fairly large cast with at least one actable little scene."[4] The cast is deployed operatically in duets, quartets, small assemblies, and large choruses, with most of the peaks of excitement or tension coinciding with the largest groupings. Jennet, the lady of the title, does not appear until well over halfway through the first act, and at first it is Thomas's unsuccessful applications to be hanged and the brothers' conflict for the hand of Alizon that vie for the audience's attention. Indeed Thomas is only half in the action at first because he is mainly "nodding in" (2:122) through the big garden window. Having outlined his demands to Richard, the clerk, he is thus an occasional third at the conversation in which Richard and Alizon get acquainted, but noise, confusion, and suspense begin to build up with the arrival of Nicholas, claiming to have killed his brother, a report that is grossly exaggerated.

This is more structurally complex than Fry's previous plays (*The Firstborn* is as demanding but is more unified) and shows the careful planning of "what scene follows another, what character goes and what character enters" (*An Experience of Critics*, 26). Nonetheless, the early effacement of Thomas was used as evidence for Fry's being deficient in the rhythms of action, an accusation also made of Eliot. Yet a character is not necessarily ineffective if he is not speaking or involved in business; Fry has not made Thomas enter later or go offstage on some pretext but has kept him before the audience's eyes dramatically, in reserve. His wish to be hanged is a single and limited gesture, which depends on its shock value and ought not to be dulled by overstatement, but his presence makes the most of the potential of this gesture. Thomas's reserve, like Jennet's late entrance, is a husbanding of resources.

The pattern of the first act is that more and more of the family—Margaret, Humphrey, and the mayor Tyson himself—enter and try to disentangle Nicholas's assertiveness while Thomas looks on, mostly silently. While Nicholas and Richard go out briefly to look for Humphrey, Thomas moves again to the foreground and in a duet with Margaret puts forward not only his own outrageous request but the hideousness of the witch-hunt he has observed, insisting on a moral reaction and developing the theme ready for Jennet's appearance. Thomas's next irruption is after Tyson's entry, when he dominates the now assembled family with persistence, noise, and ingenuity in his effort to establish officially his claim to have murdered Old Skipps, before the witch-hunt can use Skipps as evidence against its victim. This climactic shouting match is trumped in spades by a climax of a different kind—the unexpected entry of the beautiful and disheveled Jennet, effectively imposing silence and attention on characters and audience alike. Nicholas and Humphrey had just been sent out to wash, so their separate reentries mean that the impact of Jennet's beauty on them can be individually registered.

The tension is not relaxed here, for Jennet's assumption of safety and her mockery of the magic arts attributed to her are received with fear and hostility by the Tyson family, as we, but not at first Jennet, perceive from their reactions. The final climax of Act 1 occurs as Jennet finally becomes frightened and Thomas explodes in a last unavailing attempt to divert the accusation on to himself, adding for good measure the claim to be the devil and that the end of the world will take place that evening "at twenty-two forty hours precisely" (2:148). Nothing has been resolved, so the act ends with a dying fall and Jennet's helpless question, "What will happen?" (2:150), as she is imprisoned in the cellar.

Act 3 repeats this accumulative buildup of characters and excitement, but act 2 is by contrast altogether more subdued in tone. Tyson's plan that Thomas and Jennet be left alone together so that eavesdroppers—himself, Humphrey, the household's gentle, musical old chaplain, and the enormous cynical Justice Tappercoom—can listen for supernatural incrimination is a good enough device to bring the two victims onstage by themselves without change of set. Thomas and Jennet have been put to the thumbscrew, Jennet is tearstained and weary, and the atmosphere is naturally miserable though Thomas is trying hard to cheer her up: "For God's sake, shall we laugh?" (2:165). There is dramatic space for Thomas and Jennet to develop their love for each other and incidentally for Thomas to voice the arguments against fact and for a natural life force. Only when the eavesdroppers burst in on more of Jennet's ambiguous, and thus incriminating, mockery of black magic does the temperature abruptly rise. Infuriated, Thomas fells Humphrey and threatens the chaplain with his own viol; Jennet faints, and the sense of catastrophe is averted again only by Thomas and Jennet's agreeing to the chaplain's improbable experiment. That is, he thinks that Thomas will be reconciled to life by compulsory participation in Humphrey and Alizon's decorously festive betrothal party.

Because the festivity is so decorous as to be stunningly boring, act 3 begins on a low, not to say flat, note. "O tedium, tedium, tedium" (2:179), remarks Thomas to Humphrey, another refugee from the party. They are soon joined by Nicholas. The act develops through a series of short dialogues, mainly between two people, in the course of which the secondary lovers, Alizon and Richard, declare their love and decide to elope, and Humphrey tries to blackmail Jennet into bed with him as the price of her release. Gradually a climax of many characters builds up, as in the other acts, this time, however, achieving a resolution. Most significant, Richard and Alizon return from their elopement to produce Old Skipps, alive and well and in human form. The young lovers do not lose by their generosity, and they slip away again, as the gathering unwinds itself and disperses, Nicholas and Humphrey suitably escorting away the unruly Skipps, Margaret once more pursuing Alizon, until Tappercoom, fatigued, washes his hands of the whole business and also rolls away. At last Thomas allows Jennet to reconcile him to life, and they escape together.

The original idea of the play was found in an old collection of German short stories. Fry was not looking for any particular type of plot but was drawn to this one when he read it: "When you find a plot that you think will do—or rather which you are suddenly sure is exactly what you want, then that means there are elements in it that respond to what, within yourself, you are wanting to say." The story, "Wooing the Gallows" by W. Heinrich von Riehl, gives the main plot outline of an obstreperous young man who wants to be hanged and a suspected witch who does not want to be burned.[5] The young man, Jörg, claims to have murdered a traveling peddler and a foreign Jew and demands to be hanged by the town council of Nördlingen, where the murder took place. However, there is, as with Thomas Mendip, "no actual evidence of the crime to be found." Suspecting a hoax, the council put him to "that most unrelenting test of truth, the rack," but this produces only a further list of unproved robberies. Jörg is imprisoned next to a witch, the "well to do childless widow of an innkeeper," who is not young and beautiful like Jennet but "an old hag." The narrator comments that "a wealthy witch is a rarity" but explains that the bonfire-happy town council had burned all the poor old women, so "at last it came to be the turn of the young handsome and rich women as well," a suggestion for the development of *The Lady's Not for Burning*. The woman is determined and defiant, as is shown in her resistance to fifty-eight bouts of torture and in her religion, her prayers being "passionate commands rather than petitions." Jörg, impressed, admits to her that he has chosen the gallows "to put a showy end to life" because "life was a burden to him, but to take his own life and be found later in the water or the woods like a beast, was not to his taste." Hereafter the denouement differs from Fry's as it is the old woman's courage that saves herself and Jörg. He assists her escape, but she pauses only to summon her powerful friends from Ulm and returns to confront the council. In a dramatic courtroom scene, which Fry decided not to use, her firmness elicits Jörg's recantation of his false confession, and she takes him away to Ulm to "adopt him in a child's stead."

The change of the witch into a beautiful young woman who stands in a love relationship to the hero rather than in a quasi-maternal relationship is a straightforward one and has the effect of supplying love interest to the plot. More fundamental is the removal of dynamism and initiative from the heroine, for Jennet is not a defiant, aggressive heroine. It is easier to observe this than to explain where the motive force of *Lady* is to be found. And this may be the reason that critics were baffled in their search for a plot: the fates of Thomas and Jennet seem to be decided by chance, not by their own exertions, or indeed by villainy or heroism on anyone else's part. Things seem just to happen, but their happening is evidence of what Fry wants to say about human nature and the place of people in the world: it is not, on the whole, affected by defiant activism and willpower. In spite of the destructive, bloodthirsty impulses of humanity, goodness emerges as a natural, if deeply buried, part of the average human being, and life, if left alone, exerts its own pressures on the development of humanity.

A related major theme is the conflict between Thomas's conviction that life is not worth living and Jennet's tolerant self-preservation. Thomas appears with a contempt for "the damned world" and a particular disgust for humanity, both in the flesh—"Guts, humours, ventricles, nerves, fibres / And fat—the arterial labyrinth, body's hell" (2:118)—and in the spirit, in that "the blind alleys / Which they think are their immortal souls" transform the citizens into "human bloodhounds" baying for death. Thomas knows there is a witch-hunt going on, but he is the only person to be concerned. Margaret refuses to "be disturbed" at the thought of the victim, assumed to be some "wicked sobbing old woman," and Hebble later apologizes for his misgivings at burning the beautiful Jennet as

> Humanity,
> That's all, Tappercoom; it's perfectly proper
> No one is going to let it interfere
> With anything serious. I use it with great
> Discretion, I assure you.
>   (2:152)

Whether bloodthirsty or callous, the population of Cool Clary is displayed as eminently justifying Thomas's disillusion with humanity. His rejection of matter in its human form takes on the imagery of a dance of death:

> a perambulating
> Vegetable, patched with inconsequential
> Hair, looking out of two small jellies for the means
> Of life, balanced on folding bones, my sex
> No beauty but a blemish to be hidden
> Behind judicious rags . . .
>
> (2:173)

But conversely Jennet has an answer to Thomas's complaints:

> By a quirk
> Of unastonished nature, your obscene
> Decaying figure of vegetable fun
> Can drag upon a woman's heart, as though
> Heaven were dragging up the roots of hell.
>
> (2:174)

And the comic gyrations of Hebble's family in both action and dialogue make a cheerful counterpoint to the saturnine Thomas's commentary and Jennet's more pathetic fear of death. The alternation of melancholy and farce is one reason for the play's categorization as "a Spring Comedy" when Fry planned his set of four seasonal comedies, in which mood, season, and philosophy are united. *Lady* is set in spring, with the characteristic English spring conditions of rapidly alternating sun and shower, budding and growth of vegetation, and the mating of birds and animals. As Alizon says of the effect of brilliant sun reflecting from raindrops, "I've an April blindness" (2:120), and the young characters are blindly and dazzlingly led by the feverish pressure to love and be loved.

Another theme that emerges from the conflict of Thomas's and Jennet's philosophies is that of the more generous versus the more vicious feelings of human nature—the heart against savage superstition. Irrational superstition stupidly drives the populace to pointless destruction, and Margaret's refusal to "be disturbed" confirms the failure of Thomas's "last poor gamble / On the human heart" (2:128). Jennet has been frightened by "what, in their innocence, / Those old credulous children in the street / Imagine of me" (2:142) but considers this an aberration in an essentially sane world. Only

gradually does she come to realize that it is discouragingly normal for everyone to "knuckle and suckle at the big breast of irrational fears" (2:142), and
her appeals to reason are useless. Jennet's rationality as the daughter of a
primitive scientist, "a man who believed the universe was governed / By certain laws" (2:149), is a reaction against her father's later decline into alchemi-
cal superstition: "I am Jennet Jourdemayne / And I believe in the human
mind" (2:142), she announces. This a red herring for her and the audience;
the human mind has no part to play in this story, and Thomas rightly notes
that she is basing her life on delusion. It is not the human mind but the humanity at first denied by Hebble that eventually prompts Justice
Tappercoom to connive at Jennet's escape: "If she wishes to return to her cell,
no one / Can object. On the other hand—How very empty / The streets
must be just now" (2:210). Unlike the source story, it is not Jennet's own de-
nials that have won justice for her nor was it the dramatic plot twist whereby
her "crime" of turning Old Skipps into a dog is refuted by Skipps's appearance alive and singing. Tappercoom's monumental inertia, plus the wine he
has imbibed, plus his residual human kindness—"I'm too amiable tonight /
To controvert any course of events whatever" (2:207)—come to her rescue.

Humanity in the sense of actual human beings is Thomas's prime objec-
tion to the universe, and his disapproval is unqualified. He is more ambiva-
lent about nature. He may see himself as "a black and frosted rosebud"
(2:120) and describe twilight in terms of "a glittering smear, the snail-trail of
the sun" (2:164), but he later admits "something condones the world, incorrigibly" (2:190). His sheer contradictoriness—or compassion—toward
Jennet's prosaism produces an inconsistently approving paean to the
universe:

> Horns, what a waste of effort it has been
> To give you Creation's vast and exquisite
> Dilemma! where altercation thrums
> In every granule of the Milky Way,
> Persisting still in the dead-sleep of the moon,
> And heckling itself hoarse in that hot-head
> The sun.
>
> (2:169)

He draws comparisons between nature and humanity, people being

> driven and scorched
> By boomerang rages and lunacies which never

> Touch the accommodating artichoke
> Or the seraphic strawberry beaming in its bed.
>
> (2:173)

In this jocular image we have a reference to the philosophy of man's and nature's relations to God's purposes suggested in and expressed later in *Venus Observed.* The crucial reference comes as Thomas tries to alleviate Jennet's fear of oblivion:

> Nothing can be seen
> In the thistle-down, but the rough-head thistle comes.
> Rest in that riddle. I can pass to you
> Generations of roses in this wrinkled berry.
> There: now you hold in your hand a race
> Of summer gardens, it lies under centuries
> Of petals. What is not, you have in your palm.
> Rest in the riddle, rest; why not?
>
> (2:171)

This speech refers again to the concept of nature as the realization of a foreordained plan that gives assurance and completeness to plants and animals; each exists according to the essence fully laid down for it. The simple reproduction of roses and thistles proceeds without need of elaboration; the artichoke and strawberry fulfill their natures without necessity for angst or aspiration. Merlin had fancifully imagined the plan as laid down in the eternal rocks, though deriving from a reality beyond even the rocks. Thomas here is pointing out that the future is printed on the genes of the plant, to be expanded by time into an inevitable fulfillment. Only human beings have no finally fixed nature; certainly they are imprinted with certain physical characteristics and practical limitations, but their eternal dissatisfaction is a sign that this is not enough. People do not feel complete and are likely, like Thomas, to be left wandering with an unfulfilled longing for something more than physical development—life, death, love, the sense of being at home in the universe. In *Thor* the solution lay in doing the will of the One God. In this play, Thomas does not reach an explicitly metaphysical answer. He falls in love with Jennet, and the destiny the life force intends for him, as with Hoel, is not voluntarily sought. He has to accept love as the equivalent of the biological destiny of the vegetable world, as forceful for him as for thistle and rose: "I know my limitations. / When the landscape goes to seed, the wind is obsessed / By tomorrow" (2:212). And in fact, as *Venus Observed* makes clearer, the unselfish romantic union of man and woman is one way of arriving at a true sense of purpose.

The manipulation of several different plot threads represents an advance in complexity on the earlier plays. It is true that *The Firstborn* included a kind of subplot in the materialist rebellion of Shendi, but there are many more separate and more varied interest groups in *Lady*. In practical terms, the chaplain has little to do with the plot mechanism, and one might also wonder why there need to be two dispensers of justice and two young brothers, but Fry includes all of these to make specific points about the range of human nature and motivation, as well as to exploit the comic interaction of the large cast.

As appropriate to a spring comedy, the young lovers are the most generous and full of human kindness. Richard is in the painful position of being newly in love with Alizon and having to observe her betrothal to Humphrey, but he pities the plight of Jennet and Thomas. Because of his depression, he drinks three glasses of the guests' wine and ventures to defy his master, the mayor, in defending the prisoners who are being tortured:

> Those two, sir, the prisoners,
> What are you doing with them? I don't know why
> I keep calling you Sir. I'm not feeling respectful.
> If only inflicted pain could be as contagious
> As a plague, you might use it more sparingly.
>   (2:158)

Alizon reveals under her convent-bred ingenuousness—"Men are strange. It's almost unexpected / To find they speak English" (2:123)—a demure sense of irony, shown in her account of her father's problems in seeking husbands for her five elder sisters:

> and so he made up his mind
> To simplify matters and let me marry God.
> He gave me to a convent. . . .
> But he found that husbands fell into my sisters' laps.
> So then he stopped thinking of God as eligible—
> No prospects, he thought.
>   (2:122)

Her kind heart appears early in her comment on the decision that Jennet must be arrested: "Oh, must she, must she?" (2:139). And after a long spell of silence, during which she impresses the other characters as "pale, tearful" (2:180), and a "sad little soul" (2:195), she reemerges decisively bent on running away, preferably with Richard, from the Tyson family: "I'm not able to love them. / Have you forgotten what they mean to do / Tomorrow?" (2:191). Later, risking the success of this escape by returning with Old Skipps, she triumphantly explains: "We had to come back, you see, because nobody now / Will be able to burn her" (2:207)

The love of Alizon and Richard is a generous love, not narrowly selfish like that of the brothers Humphrey and Nicholas. Humphrey exemplifies physical love, as his businesslike approach to Jennet shows: "it's give and take, the basis / Of all understanding" (2:198). His answer to Jennet's appeal, "Doesn't my plight seem pitiable to you?" (2:200), returns straight to his own physical sensations: "Pitiable, yes. It makes me long for you / Intolerably" (2:200). Nicholas, just as self-centered, is, however, motivated by romantic and imaginative trappings. He loves Alizon because she has the forbidden charm of being Humphrey's betrothed:

> I loved her once—earlier today—
> Loved her with a passionate misapprehension.
> I thought you wanted her, and I'm always deeply
> Devoted to your affairs. But now I'm bored.
>
> (2:180)

Then his attraction to Jennet is fired by her supposed exotic infernal powers, as well as her effect on Humphrey:

> I feel such tenderness for you, not only because
> I think you've bewitched my brother, which would be
> A most salutary thing, but because, even more
> Than other women, you carry a sense of that cavernous
> Night folded in night, where Creation sleeps
> And dreams of men. If only we loved each other
> Down the pitshaft of love I could go
> To the motive mysteries under the soul's floor.
> Well drenched in damnation I should be as pure
> As a limewashed wall.
>
> (2:196)

The inward-turned emotions of the two brothers fail to engage with the objects of their attention, and this says little for their maturity or humanity.

Tyson, the mayor, is less honest than Humphrey in neither expressing nor exorcising his hidden lusts. The subtext of his first reaction to Alizon,

> So this is the young lady? Very nice, very charming.—
> And a very pretty dress.
> Splendid material, a florin a yard
> If a groat,
>
> (2:133)

is that he cannot resist getting his hands on her under the pretext of examining her dress material. Jennet also fascinates him, so that his maudlin reaction is to cry, "We must burn her, / Before she destroys our reason," shrewdly queried by Justice Tappercoom as an effort "to get rid of temptation, / Tyson? A belated visit of the wanton flesh / After all these years?" (2:187). Thomas in his role as scourge of humanity accuses him of living entirely by negative repressions:

> Your love
> Is the fear of being alone; your world's history
> The fear of a possible leap by a possible antagonist
> Out of a possible shadow.
>
> (2:143)

Tyson also may have a financial motive for his obduracy. Thomas originally suggested, "He can see she's a girl of property / And the property goes to the town if she's a witch" (2:139), and Tappercoom certainly finds this a reason for ignoring humane feelings:

> And tomorrow, remember, you'll have her property
> Instead of your present longing for impropriety.
> And her house, now I come to think of it,
> Will suit me nicely.
>
> (2:189)

Tappercoom is a man who, appropriate to his mountainous size, prefers not to "be disturbed" by anything. If he is not actively benevolent, however, he is not, on the other hand, malign. His inertia finally, under the influence of alcohol, becomes passive benevolence: "I'm too amiable to-night / To controvert any course of events whatsoever" (2:207). And in trying to avoid further inconvenience, he suggests Jennet's escape. The "certain mildness in the night," the "kind of somnolent inattention" (2:210) is in him as much as in the atmosphere. Like Margaret, he represents a blinkered, self-interested human nature that does good rather by chance than for sufficient reasons.

Justice and administration are devoid of positive virtues but ramble to a happy ending. The church, as represented by the chaplain, is also less than positive. The chaplain's ineffectiveness as a dramatic character—his contribution is to the texture of the comedy rather than to the plot—is in fact the point of his role. Fry says, "I put him in to show the ineffectuality of the Church. It means well but does nothing." The following speech is characteristically benevolent and self-deprecating:

> Ah . . . ah . . . I'm not really here. I came
> For my angel, a foolish way to speak of it,
> This instrument. May I say, a happy issue
> Out of all your afflictions? I hope so.—Well,
> I'm away now.
>
> (2:163)

He is a charming character, but even though he has not the self-deceiving hypocrisy of Tyson, he fails to act according to his spiritual function. "Do you think he knows / What has been happening to us?" asks Jennet after their torture. And Thomas pinpoints the chaplain's weakness: "He knows all right. But he's subdued / To the cloth he works in" (2:164). Not only is the chaplain a weak personality but the cloth, the ecclesiastical profession, is itself subservient to the pressures of the civil community.

Margaret similarly has no motives, overt or repressed, for wishing ill to Jennet, but neither does she express any interest in her fate. Fry planned Margaret as exclusively domestic, the housewife who stubbornly refuses to concern herself with anything outside her own household, and we note that her excitement over the fall of a burning log from the hearth contrasts with her indifference to the burning of a human being. Her managing of her children and brother, though massively self-confident, is less dominating than nannylike; however, like Tappercoom and the chaplain, she is of the large majority of humanity who prefer to turn a blind eye to evil and injustice that do not affect them.

Finally, Old Skipps is the disreputable old man who appears only at the end of the play, though he has been much discussed as the pivotal supposed victim of both Jennet's witchcraft and Thomas's murder. As a deus ex machina he is inconclusive. Jennet is not triumphantly vindicated by his appearance but has to steal away, abandoning all she has. Skipps does at least show up the dubious and spurious nature of all the attacks on Jennet, though the audience has had little doubt about these during the action. His appearance otherwise provides a parody of the illusions of the rest of the play. Thomas and Nicholas tease him that he is known to be dead, and the drunken and credulous old man assumes he is among the saints in heaven. His supernatural illusion is as foolish as Jennet's supposed witchcraft or Thomas's claims to be the devil.

Jennet, the eponymous heroine of the play, is a character of some depth. She and many of the other characters—Alizon, Jennet, Devizes, Jourdemayne—take their names from a famous Lancashire witchcraft trial of the seventeenth century. *Jourdemayne* particularly gave Fry the scope to play upon the meanings of *jour*, "today," and *demain*, "tomorrow." We see Thomas capitulate in the end to the pressures of tomorrow: "When the landscape goes to seed the wind is obsessed / By tomorrow" (2:212). Because Jennet is so unlike the defiant widow of Fry's source, but at the same time is no ingenue like Alizon, she has to make her impression on the audience in other ways. Like the April setting, Jennet is both bright and dark, sunny and melancholy, witty and earnest. As an anachronistic forerunner of the Enlightenment, Jennet proclaims her belief in the human mind and is evidently mistaken in that belief insofar as it applies to the townsfolk of Cool Clary, but she still persists in challenging Thomas's "devilry":

> And so, for me the actual!
> What I touch, what I see, what I know; the essential fact . . .
> And, if I may say it
> Without appearing rude, absolutely
> No devils.
>
>   (2:168)

But she has to learn, alongside Thomas, that the actual is "the bare untruth." He points out to her that what her senses show her is merely "appearances": "what greater superstition / Is there than the mumbo-jumbo of believing / In reality?" (2:169). And indeed her love for him is based on mystery: "the magnetism of mystery / And your curious passion for death. You are making yourself / A breeding-ground for love and must take the consequences" (2:172). The result is that her love sweeps away her rationalism: "Something compels us into / The terrible fallacy that man is desirable / And there's no escaping into truth" (2:174).

Therefore in act 3 she reappears praising the beauty of the moon and the legend of the queen of Sheba and seeing the whole of creation in the web of a spider, changed by mortality and love. Instead of concentrating her human mind wonderfully, the prospect of execution is liberating her imagination. Nonetheless, she is no more a Joan of Arc than she is a virago, and her fear, when weakness and tiredness make her burst into tears and when she faints at threat of the fire, engages the audience's sympathy at a realistic and human level of response. At these points, in spite of the comic tone, the evil and enormity of her persecution are seriously present for the audience. Therefore when Humphrey approaches her with his bargain of escape from the flames by complying with his lust, her dilemma is felt as far from frivolous. The pragmatic, skeptical girl has acquired new values with love but fully apprehends the penalty of upholding them. The simple choice of death or dishonor has in her case taken the form of "what is life for?" She says, "I seem to wish to have some importance in the play of time" (2:200), a newly abstract, fanciful importance in the context of her earlier matter-of-factness. Either there is a purpose, to which her death will contribute, or if there is no purpose, her death will be still a meaningful protest, a call to God for some sign, some help. Like a Shakespearean heroine, Jennet is brave enough to endure all but physical violence and even to modulate from earnestness back to rueful humor as a means of enduring anxiety—"Though, on the other hand, I admit it might / Be immensely foolish" (2:200).

The character of Thomas is dynamic in spite of his negative ambitions, and in fact his course of action has a hidden positive motive, which Jennet finally discerns:

> There was a soldier,
> Discharged and centreless, with a towering pride
> In his sensibility, and an endearing
> Disposition to be a hero, who wanted
> To make an example of himself to all
> Erring mankind, and falling in with a witch-hunt
> His good heart took the opportunity
> Of providing a diversion.
>
> (2:206)

Thomas will not admit this, and there is no proof of Jennet's partial diagnosis, but this was the motive Fry intended Thomas to have: he has heard the rumor of the witch-hunt in the tavern and tried to preempt the Old Skipps accusation before he knew who the "witch" was—a truly disinterested piece of quixotry, though his disgust with the world and willingness to leave it are genuine enough. The benevolent impulse replaces the arbitrary distaste for being "found in a ditch" of the original short story hero and replaces the courage of the "heroine" as a positive theme of the action. Fry says he had in mind the kind of discharged, disillusioned soldier who could be seen tramping the roads after any major war. Thomas's mention of "floundering in Flanders for the past seven years" (2:136) will remind the audience of the traumatic experiences of a generation in World War I.

He has to be at the same time terminally disgusted with the world, ready to make his own death useful to an unknown victim, forceful enough to impose his will—or nearly—on the townsfolk, and eminently likable. Richard says, "I like you as much as I've liked anybody" (2:118), and even Humphrey growls, "I strongly resent finding you slightly pleasant" (2:179). A satiric inextinguishable articulacy is the main way the character achieves all this, and by a series of unexpected speeches, Thomas dominates the cast, even against no little competition from the other eccentrics of Cool Clary. As plot and theme develop together, Thomas's kind action involves him again in human life, decry though he may. His love for Jennet makes it impossible for him in the end to abandon her along with the rest of the world. At first, struggling, he says, "Let the world / Go, lady, it isn't worth the candle" (2:150), but soon, in spite of his anxiety not to be trapped by love, he finds himself musing, "Something condones the world, incorrigibly" (2:190), and realizes he has taken on Jennet's new enchanted vision of beauty, and for the same reason. Forced to admit his love for Jennet, he begs her to save herself; still claiming death for himself, he no longer recommends it for her, an evident weakening of his absolute antilife stance. This is, in fact, a consistency within inconsistency because Thomas's objections to humanity, appearing in his urging Margaret to "be disturbed," are based on its lack of human kindness, which in turn proves that this is a quality he greatly prizes.

Nonetheless, Thomas does not change his abrasive character because of being in love. Certainly he finds a reason to go on living in that he happens to have been fortunate enough to have met and loved Jennet, but he stubbornly persists in rejecting everything else:

> Girl, you haven't changed the world.
> Glimmer as you will, the world's not changed.
> I love you, but the world's not changed. Perhaps
> I could draw you up over my eyes for a time
> But the world sickens me still.
>
> (2:211)

When Fry directed a touring production of *Lady* in 1970, he was concerned particularly with stressing the realism of Thomas's disillusion, in the sense that he was in truth deeply alienated by the real evil evident in human life, displayed in the raw in the mud of Flanders, and which had been brought home to Fry and his generation in World War II. On a small scale, it was to be found also in the blind callousness of English countryfolk. Unless this chord of genuine despair is brought out in production, Thomas's gesture may appear merely theatrical. His role is so articulate, assertive, and witty that he is not seen as withdrawing from the humanity he despises. If, then, the part is exploited only for its dominant theatricality, as a source of verbal fireworks, the satiric aspect is overlooked, and conversely, if the character is modified by a melancholy air, the motivating assertiveness is lost. In the first Arts Theatre production, Alec Clunes tended more to the vivid, frivolous interpretation. T. C. Worsley said, "He speaks the poetry admirably; he moves expressively; he gives to the character warmth, virility, light, colour, movement: he gives it everything except life and he would give it that if it were there to give."[6] In the following West End revival, John Gielgud toned down his performance as appropriate to a young man with a death wish and, according to the *Times* seemed "seldom to be quite at the centre of the stage."[7] Although Thomas is conceived as quite a young man, "in his late twenties, perhaps," professional actors have tended to be fortyish; Kenneth Branagh in a 1987 television production was the nearest to the right age and was praised for his dangerous desperation under the savage persiflage.

Although Fry has a clear idea of certain effects that he wanted and is exasperated by productions noticeably in conflict with the text—as when Jennet's apologies for looking "unruly" and "shamefully near a flood of tears" are delivered by an actress of cheerful demeanor and pristine neatness—he never makes his stage directions very specific because he feels that directors should have some freedom in interpretation. Therefore, the smartness and lightness of the first productions were in a way adjusting themselves to their audience without any intention of twisting the text. It may be that the success of Fry's seasonal comedies conquered the West End for poetic drama, but West End productions may have erased some of their individuality and sense of values.

The importance of commercial success should not be overlooked. Of the second production that Gielgud directed as well as acted in, T. C. Worsley, improving his first impression of the play, pointed out that "to have risked putting on a play that is, on the face of it, so little commercial, with so excellent a cast and with such style (the decor is by Oliver Messel) is a great credit to all responsible." The attitude of the time, as well as the effect of *Lady* on audiences, is helpfully set out in his next comment: "The general public, faced with the prospect of a comedy in verse, suspects, with some justice as a general rule, that it is going to be embarrassed and bored. I should like to try and convince them that at *The Lady's Not for Burning* at the Globe they will be neither—if one may judge from the almost continuous ripple of amusement, punctuated by frequent outbursts of laughter, which greeted it on the second night. It is enormously high-spirited and quite un-precious."[8] Significantly, verse drama was not expected to be popular, an assumption crucial to Eliot's dramatic writing; nonetheless Fry's play demonstrably was very popular. More even than *Phoenix, Lady* invited critical reaction to Fry's language, somehow more insistent now that eleven characters rather than two or three shared it. Another critic was surprised at the audience's appreciation of "so sophisticated a work," by which he meant that the play depended "on subtleties and satire and on the superb extravagance of its language."[9]

One of the signs that the play is not trying to conceal its extravagant language is that some characters draw attention to their linguistic virtuosity. An early hint of Thomas's continuing engagement with the world is his ready profuseness of speech. He is not too world weary to take the trouble of amazing Richard with a set-piece description of his home: "A castle as draughty as a tree. At every sunset / It falls into the river and fish swim through its walls" (2:118). Then he accuses Richard of recklessness in seeking his as yet unknown fate:

> you're desperate
> To fly into any noose of the sun that should dangle
> Down from the sky. Life, forbye, is the way
> We fatten for the Michaelmas of our own particular
> Gallows.
>
> (2:119)

He then comments complacently on his verbal performance, "What a wonderful thing is metaphor" (2:119), encouraging the audience too to note and admire the play's style.

In this play, Fry's poetic effect mainly relies on imagery, the associated sounds of words, and the exploitation of various different meanings and not so much on rhythm (and not at all on rhyme). Imagery far outweighs the other two and even more than in *Phoenix* is of the surprising kind of conceit that draws attention to the speaker's—or writer's—cleverness. Tappercoom's epigram on a shooting star forces unlikes into likeness in this way: "An excess of phlegm / In the solar system. It was on its way / To a heavenly spitoon" (2:155). He underlines the "cleverness" by adding happily, "How is that? How is that?" (2:155). He tells the chaplain, "Let the butterflies come to you, Chaplain, / Or you'll never be pollinated into a bishop" (2:188)—a comic conceit because the aged, droopy chaplain could hardly be less flowerlike. Similarly Jennet ends the play in Shakespearean style with "That was the pickaxe voice of a cock, beginning / To break up the night" (2:212). This kind of conceit depends for its effect on standing out from the surrounding language and would lose this contrast if too many were fired off together in a series of one-liners. But most of the images are less individually highlighted and more interwoven into the developing texture of the dialogue. Fry's favorite imagery of light, water, and music recurs throughout. Moonlight, sunlight, and starlight are naturally related to beauty, love, and vitality. For example, Thomas notes the contrast of nature with the destructive "human jackals":

> Out here is a sky so gentle
> Five stars are ventured on it. I can see
> The sky's pale belly glowing and growing big,
> Soon to deliver the moon.
> (2:164)

Jennet struggles to realize the difference made by one day, measured by sun and moon:

> The morning came, and left
> The sunlight on my step like any normal
> Tradesman. But now every spark
> Of likelihood has gone. The light draws off
> As easily as though no one could die
> Tomorrow.
> (2:165)

Alizon has already set the keynote on her first appearance, in another prolonged passage pursuing several images of light:

> Coming in from the light, I am all out at the eyes.
> Such white doves were paddling in the sunshine
> And the trees were as bright as a shower of broken glass.
> Out there, in the sparkling air, the sun and the rain

> Clash together like the cymbals clashing
> When David did his dance.
>
> (2:120)

This spring comedy is thematically concerned to tell us that life is a mixture of sun and shower, but even the rain is springlike and hopeful, scattering light rather than shadow. Love gives value to life, and "love still pitches his tent of light among / The suns and moons" (2:174), Jennet claims. We know that she embodies life and love. Like Alizon she appears, creating "a sense of daylight" (2:183), and again her image for Thomas, challenging him to "shine less brightly upon yourself" (2:173), reinforces the effect of vitality noticeable under his pose of rejection.

Water and music occur separately and together. As in *Phoenix*, the sea is associated with powerful natural forces, which are often hidden. Jennet's important perception of "the human deep-sea sound" (2:200) marks her acceptance of the value of the heart and humanity, and her own transforming love for Thomas has its origins in "that inland sea, the heart" (2:184). The chaplain, unfortunately found wanting in real effectiveness, shows the better side of his nature in his desire for universal harmony, practically by his love for his viol, and poetically in his vain aspiration to the pacifying musical skill of Orpheus and his dream that the ladder to heaven is made entirely of diminished sevenths. Thomas rhetorically admits the power and harmony of nature but unites the three strands of imagery, only to argue that people are cut off from all of it:

> The spheres churned on,
> Hoping to charm our ears
> With sufficient organ-music, sadly sent out
> On the wrong wave of sound; but still they roll
> Fabulous and fine, a roundabout
> Of doomed and golden notes. And on beyond,
> Profound with thunder of oceanic power,
> Lie the morose dynamics of our dumb friend
> Jehovah.
>
> (2:148)

The point is that the local disturbance of the witch-hunt is being gently but constantly set against its macrocosmic background. As Thomas says,

> How is it we come
> To see this as a haven in the eye?

> Why should we hawk and spit out ecstasy
> As though we were nightingales, and call these quite
> Casual degrees and differences
> Beauty? What guile recommends the world
> And gives our eyes the special sense to be
> Deluded, above all animals?
>
> (2:190)

Natural beauty and harmony is prompting human beings, above all other animals, to grope for a meaning beyond the dog-eat-dog despair that has smitten Thomas, and the imagery reflects these constant promptings of nature and the macrocosm. The network of beautiful and positive imagery then counteracts, and sometimes obliterates, the theme of pain and cruelty borne mainly by Thomas and Jennet. This is important to the overall movement of the play; beauty, light, harmony, and power are all aspects of the divine plan, which overrides the individual's misgivings and, like the Shavian life force in *Man and Superman*, imposes the happy ending on Thomas, not because of the conventions of comedy but because the happy ending is a means to further the onward progression of humanity. One is not allowed to give up. One must accept what Merlin called "the very obdurate pressure / Edging men towards a shape beyond / The shape they know" (2:102).

It is true, however, that the language also expresses the pain and cruelty of life. Thomas's description of the jewels over which Jennet is brooding, though beautiful, has a melancholy cast effected by assonance and association. She has been invited to "make free with my jewel box" by Margaret, who later asks, "Where is she now?" Thomas replies:

> No doubt
> Still making free. Off she has gone,
> Away to the melting moody horizons of opal,
> Moonstone, bloodstone; now moving in lazy
> Amber, now sheltering in the shade
> Of jade from a brief rainfall of diamonds.
> Able to think to-morrow has an even
> Brighter air, a glitter less moderate,
> A quite unparalleled freedom in the fire:
> A death, no bounds to it. Where is she now?
> She is dressing, I imagine.
>
> (2:181–82)

The long vowels in the names of these jewels help the moody picture Thomas is building up. The shade is not from sun but from rainfall, and the echoing sounds of "moody," "moonstone," and "moving" change to the brisker "glitter less moderate" as he juxtaposes her jeweled beauty with the threat of a cruel death. His final simple answer to Margaret's question turns the banality of such a question into an accusation of callousness, and indeed Margaret replies, "I don't like to think of her." As in *Phoenix* and *The Firstborn*, Fry has eschewed special effects to use a kind of verse that will do for everything, but there are many variations of style and movement within speeches, as here, as well as between characters. The impression of the *Observer* critic that "these eloquent folk do not grow in the mind for the simple reason that all of them talk alike" is evidently mistaken.[10] Certainly there is a family resemblance between the dialogue of most of the characters, as there is between that of all the characters of Anton Chekhov, a different resemblance between those of John Millington Synge, or those of Shaw, and so on. But although the characters do not on the whole distinguish themselves by totally different styles of language (Old Skipps is the exception here) as in *The Boy with a Cart*, their dialogue is quite clearly differentiated. Margaret's style, for example, is simple in syntax, vocabulary, and idioms, whereas the chaplain rambles comically in chains of self-generating associations.

The characters generally show not only the eloquence that is a convention of verse drama but also the same conscious exploitation of the connotations of words as of imagery. Thomas savagely plays on words when he answers Tyson's "One God, one point of view, / A general acquiescence to the mean" by adding a second and third meaning: "And God knows when you say the mean, you mean / The mean" (2:186). On the other hand, unintentional ambiguity betrays some of the characters—for instance, when Humphrey self-centeredly says, "It would be insufferable / If you were burned before I could know you" (2:196). He is insensitive enough to use the word *insufferable* of his own feelings, not seeing that they appear insignificant beside the threat of real "suffering" facing Jennet.

Like the wit of the more extended conceits, the play on words also contributes to the humor. It is much more laborious to analyze this verbal wit than to respond to it, but a few examples will show how the mental agility involved in pursuing unexpected meanings of words is of the same kind in the comic lines and in the serious poetry. The surprise of having a word presented for understanding in one sense, quickly followed by a change of use taking it in another sense, is the technique of much of the verbal comedy. Nicholas means "fresh air outside" when he says he is taking Alizon "out into the air," but Margaret foils him by using the word more generally to mean "atmosphere" and says, "Unnecessary. / She's in the air already. This room is full of it" (125). The contrasting metaphorical and literal meanings of "born" and "reborn" similarly create a shock of comic surprise when Margaret deflates Nicholas's claim to have been reborn: "Nicholas, you always think / You can do things better than your mother. You can be sure / You were born quite adequately on the first occasion" (2:125). The deliberate use of a word like *adequately*, normally used of mundane transactions, not of birth, is characteristic of Fry's comic technique. Tyson's threat to have Thomas whipped at the cart's tail invokes comic understatement in his suggestion, "an unfortunate experience / At the cart's tail," and in Thomas's businesslike response, "Unacceptable. Hanging or nothing" (2:134). These comic cheatings of expectation occur in nearly every speech and account for the audience's "constant ripple of amusement" described by T. C. Worsley, though humor also springs from the characterization: the chaplain's bumbling, Tappercoom's large size and matching sense of self-importance, Margaret's blinkered lack of imagination (she refuses to believe that Doomsday could possibly occur in the spring: "Heaven, I am quite sure, wouldn't disappoint the bulbs" [2:148]).

The question then recurs as to whether Fry has in fact overdone the comedy and pleasant imagery as vehicles of the positive theme, to the detriment of the problems of suffering and meanness acknowledged by the plot. The structure parallels the increasingly somber tone of the play as it proceeds. At first Thomas's disillusion is both sincere and assumed—he really wants to die because he is tired of life, and he is playing the role of a man who wants to die because he is trying to save Jennet—and the role-playing aspect brings a certain exaggeration and frivolity to his presence in the early scenes. It is Jennet who brings the action near to tragedy as she is forced into real fear.

Some sequences, particularly in act 2 where Fry has taken care to allow time to emphasize the predicament of the victims, do need a slower pace, without directorial speed and business distracting from the text. However, a problem area is the presentation of the two victims' reaction to torture when they appear in act 2 after a lengthy session with the thumbscrew. In spite of Richard's outrage, the impact of inflicted pain is not usually recognized by the audience. Jennet refers to "what has been happening to us" (2:164) and later says to Thomas, "Your thumbs. / I'm sure they're giving you pain" (2:168); otherwise she complains of tiredness and fear but makes no mention of pain. As with the use of the corpse in *Phoenix,* there is an ambivalence in the writer's intention in that there is a conflict between the wish to make a forcible statement but at the same time not to break the bounds of this type of comedy, which can encompass depth of emotion but not physical horror. It would be possible to make the point in production perhaps by the liberal use of bandages and blood, but Fry felt that audiences would not be able to accept the shock of such realism in this kind of play, and to attempt it would be to write not a comedy but a problem play. It is a difficulty that Fry pursues in his next two comedies, taking in turn the fear of burning and the approach of death and giving due weight to both without moving across to tragedy or black farce.

Chapter Six

No One Is Separate from Another: *Venus Observed*

The springlike-ness of *The Lady's Not for Burning* had developed as the play was written: the autumnal nature of *Venus Observed* was an essential part of the initial concept. Says the author: "*Venus Observed* was planned as one of a series of four comedies, a comedy for each of the seasons of the year, four comedies of mood. I don't know whether a comedy of mood is an accepted category, or whether it's something I've coined to cover my particular aim. It means that the scene, the season and the characters, are bound together in one climate."[1] Briefly, the situation of *Venus Observed* shows the fifty-year-old duke of Altair resolving to settle down and marry one of his former mistresses. He is tempted away from this sensible plan by a last attempt to recapture youthfulness in the person of the twenty-five-year-old Perpetua, daughter of his bailiff, Reedbeck. The structure of *Venus* is similar to that of *Lady*, with a first act gradually introducing its characters in ones and twos, until a group of eight is gathered in the duke's observatory. The pretext is a party to watch an eclipse of the sun; the ulterior agenda, as the duke begins by explaining to the grown-up son of his first marriage, Edgar, is to choose a wife from a short list of three. Furthermore, he wants Edgar to make the decision for him—imitating the classic legend of the judgment of Paris by indicating his choice with the gift of an apple. A subplot is immediately set going in a different father and son duologue in which Dominic, Reedbeck's priggish son, privately accuses his father of long-term embezzlement of the duke's revenues, a problem planted for development later.

After this ground plan of the plot, the superstructure of characters is built up. The visitors arrive one by one: the intense, fey actress Rosabel; the large, good-natured Jessie; and the dignified, trenchant Hilda. Each lady has expected to be the only guest, and in a long speech, Rosabel indirectly reveals a long-felt sense of injury, apparently at the ending of her relationship with the duke, and particularly at his not seeming to realize her feelings, then or now. Edgar has already given her the apple, attracted by her sensitivity and charm, but now he takes it back. His second offer, to Jessie, is also destined to be abortive. The darkness of the eclipse rolls away dramatically to reveal Perpetua, Reedbeck's daughter newly returned from America, her entrance as delayed as Jennet's was, and introducing a new phase of the plot.

Both the duke and Edgar are immediately attracted to her, and the act reaches a surprising climax when some wrangling between father and son as to whether she shall be given the significant apple is arrested by an unexpected initiative by Perpetua herself. The duke holds out the apple, and, the stage direction says, "Perpetua has whipped a very small pistol from a pigskin holster at her belt. She shoots and shatters the apple. There is an incredulous, shaken silence" (1:177). She confesses that she has been a member of an aesthetic protest group and actually spent some time in prison for attacking ugly objects and buildings but, discouraged at her ineffectuality, has returned to England to try to strengthen her own identity and values before taking further action against the outside world. This sudden dynamism and the explanation shows up Perpetua as an activist rather than a victim, it introduces the motif of imprisonment, and it inspires Rosabel with emulation ready for the plot developments in act 2.

Fry would have liked to have kept to one set for the whole play, but because catastrophe is to strike the observatory, he was not able to do that, and so he alternates scenes between the observatory and the Temple of the Ancient Virtues. The latter in compensation has a symbolic function; it is the place in which some of the characters are brought back to virtues they have mislaid. As in the second act of *Lady*, act 2 advances the interests of different small groups of characters. Perpetua is tempted by Dominic to do the wrong thing for the right reason, that is, to protect their criminal father from inevitable discovery by marrying the duke herself—an echo of Humphrey's blackmail of Jennet. Perpetua agrees and obediently goes off with the duke to practice archery and flirtation. Reedbeck's fury with Dominic on discovering this plot to save him is interrupted by Jessie, coming to write her letters in the temple, where she remains as an anchor person and confessional lay figure for the rest of the scene.

First Jessie listens to Hilda's confidences about the inadequacies of her boring husband, Roderic, confidences put in perspective by the news of Roderic's having met with a hunting accident. Absentmindedly, Jessie encourages the jealous Edgar to compete with his father, now monopolizing Perpetua among the archery butts, and she is a pacifying influence on the resulting father and son conflict when Edgar's arrow in the bull's-eye passes dangerously near the duke. For the sake of the plot, however, she has not heard Perpetua's assignation to meet the duke that night in the observatory. Finally, though she gives good advice to the obsessive Rosabel at the end of the scene, she also fails to understand Rosabel's enigmatic but ominous hints: "I shall send his Observatory / Where Nero's Rome has gone" (1:206).

The audience may or may not have grasped what Rosabel intends, but as the second scene of act 2 opens with a long conversation between the duke and Perpetua in the darkened observatory, there is time to forget this threatening plot element. The darkness, the distant stars, and the supernatural—for this is Halloween—all add strangeness to what is planned by the duke as a scene of seduction. Perpetua, however, does not respond to the atmosphere and is cool to the duke's confidences. The pace quickens, and the scene becomes a fencing match between the two, with Perpetua seeming to evade the duke rather than seek to capture him. Perhaps his assurance makes her suspicious. "Why are you so sure / That I must love you?" she asks, and then, more bluntly, "Do you know anything against my father?" (1:215). The dialogue has built up to this open admission of why they are there, and Perpetua gives it a surprising culmination by refusing the duke's offer of marriage after all: "No, no, you're mistaken, and I was quite / Mistaken, too!" (1:216). Once again, she has refused to play the expected role and has asserted herself to reject the threat to her freedom. There is a dying fall to the conversation after this. The duke, though taking his rejection like a gentleman, cannot help but lament a little: "I seem to have come to the end of myself / Sooner than I expected" (1:217). It seems as though the scene is going to end with a whimper, but abruptly Fry launches it into a different orbit as the two notice that the house is on fire.

One might think at first that this development is designed to reverse the melancholy separation we have just seen, for Perpetua panics as the flames destroy the staircase, and she flings herself into the duke's arms, hysterically agreeing to love him in the desperation of her fear. This moment of tension must, of course, be resolved by a rescue, and on cue the duke's servant, Reddleman, floats up the remainder of the burned staircase claiming that an escape route still exists. Fry then characteristically overtops his own climax by producing a second rescuer as Bates, another servant, enters through the window from a ladder. The comic menservants wrangle over the right to rescue one prisoner each, and apparently the act has culminated in a premature happy ending.

The last and shortest act, in the Temple of the Ancient Virtues, reverses the solution of the exciting fire scene. It begins in darkness, except for the reflections of the fire in the lake, and Rosabel, weeping in solitude, is the only character on stage. Here *Venus* differs structurally from *Lady* in that apart from a brief return of the guests, there is no grand assembly of the entire cast for a denouement. Instead, the series of small groupings continues, with Rosabel confessing first to Dominic and then to the duke that she deliberately started the fire. Dominic's guilt at having indirectly put Perpetua in such a dangerous situation does not prevent his sitting in judgment on Rosabel and suggesting that she give herself up to the local constable. Even more remorseful after the duke receives her confession with rather absentminded lamentations for his observatory, she hurries off to do penance.

Perpetua is equally unable to make the duke attend to her feelings. The audience can see that she has something important to tell him, but it is delayed by the interruptions of Bates, Reddleman, Reedbeck, and Dominic, so her repeated "Oh do let me speak to you!" holds this series of interruptions together in suspense for her eventual revelation. The servants are soon disposed of, and the duke, triumphant, he thinks, in his successful love, makes equally short work of Reedbeck's confession of his thefts. As Dominic summarizes it, the duke has "noticed the discrepancies and legalised them" (1:234). His jubilation is so characteristically voluble that Perpetua finally has to stem him in full flow and recant her former declaration of love more firmly and publicly than she had intended. As in the previous scene, the climactic shock is followed effectively by a plunge into gloom and pathos. The tone can hardly be retrieved by another fire, and in fact the duke's brave recovery is followed by a more significant change of heart. His speech of forgiveness regains eloquence and buoyancy and ends in humor:

> I forgive
> Everything, my most dear Perpetua,
> Except that I wasn't born something less ambitious.
> Such as a Muscovy duck.
>
> (1:237)

But the simultaneous arrival of the other anxious guests, and especially Hilda's account of her husband, Roderic, or, more exactly, her account of her renewed respect and wonder at Roderic's human uniqueness, triggers in the duke the sudden thought that Rosabel is hurt. This is an important turning point—he is at last thinking of someone other than himself, and the implications of Rosabel's confession belatedly come home to him; she has "loved me beyond her strength . . . Excellent, blessed Rosabel" (1:241).

The stage begins to empty, and Perpetua is now left alone with Edgar to make some apology for having lied to him while seeking to entangle his father. It is only a tentative love scene in spite of Edgar's ready forgiveness, for Perpetua is preoccupied and chastened by the inevitable pain her self-assertion has caused. She realizes that pursuing integrity often impinges unpleasantly on someone else. But this is an autumn comedy, and the fate of young lovers belongs to the spring. They are replaced by the duke and Reedbeck, although Reedbeck is a half-asleep sounding board for the duke, who launches into what is at first a lamentation on his world—"a unison / Of aging . . . all decaying"—but characteristically ends with the silver lining, "How fortunate to grow in the crow-footed woods" (1:245). Soon he is in full enthusiastic spate again—"how marvellous it is to moulder"—and this celebration of the autumn landscape—"How in a field of milk-white haze the lost / Apollo glows and wanders towards noon" (1:246)—takes in his own physical aging, accepted at last. At the same time, he announces that he intends to marry Rosabel, thus accomplishing the process interrupted at the beginning of the play. Then he had been less than enthusiastic about Edgar's choice for him, but now he has learned the lesson she, in particular, wanted to teach him. The ends of the ring have perhaps joined after all, and the duke and Rosabel, "sharing two solitudes" (1:247) will escape from the loneliness of the human condition.

The movement of the play, then, is designed to follow the careers of the duke and Perpetua, with particular emphasis on the former, who is the seasonal hero, the autumnal duke. He bears most of the weight of the philosophic message of *Venus*, both explicitly and as demonstrated through his character and its eventual development. Charming and generally benevolent, he is accused by Rosabel, with some justice, of living under an "impervious umbrella of satisfaction" (1:169). His justification seems to be that he is obliged to pay no more attention to his immediate circle—though no less—than to the rest of humanity. This has been evident from the opening when he handed over the choice of wife to his son: "Shall I be happy on Tuesdays, Thursdays, and Saturdays, / Or on Mondays, Wednesdays, and Fridays? Some such difference / Is all that your choice involves" (1:151).

The duke has carried Fry's theme of appreciation of the amazing variety of the universe rather too far. He says all the right things about the uniqueness of his past love affairs, but this equal evaluation extends to all womankind, to the beauties of inanimate nature, and to the most distant features of the cosmos he surveys from his observatory. Rosabel was right in seeing that this apportioning of equal value to everything gives no true value to anything. The duke maintains his comfortable detachment by refusing to engage his emotions with any one particular thing. Loneliness has prompted him to seek refuge from "year after year, flocks of girls" (1:150). Loneliness, however, is in effect the result of a lack of engagement with other people, especially with one particular person, and as long as his remarriage is an arbitrary, detached gesture, it will not solve the problem.

Loneliness also is a general condition of human beings, and the duke is perceptive enough to see beyond his own wifeless condition to the loneliness of all human detachment from the much appreciated, much observed universe around him. In his more confident, aesthetic way, he is expressing the same sense of being a stranger in the world that Cymen felt in *Thor*. In a central speech he says:

> Over all the world
> Men move unhoming, and eternally
> Concerned: a swarm of bees who have lost their queen.
> Nothing else is so ill at ease. We know
> How patiently the toad suns on the stone,
> How the indolent fish waves its tail in time
> With the waving weed . . .
> And the trees, when the weather is waking, quicken without
> Question, their leaves assemble in a perfect faith
> Of summer; and so with all the world's life,
> Except ours.
>
> (1:200–1)

He has a sense of the plan, the blueprint for nature that Merlin described in *Thor*, but realizes humanity is excluded. "The question," he says, "is a man's / Estrangement in a world / Where everything else conforms" (1:201). The answer, he says, is

> a complete, unsolitary life,
> Where happiness leaves no room for the restless mind
> And I, as unlaborious
> As a laburnum tree, hang in caresses of gold.
>
> (1:201)

Although one answer is, as in *Thor*, to seek God's will and unify oneself with it, another alternative is to follow God's will passively and unite fully with another human being, living with and for someone else.

Two parallels appear here. One is with a platonic idea explicated by Berdyaev, a philosopher who greatly influenced Fry's thought, that "man cannot remain in a state of division, a mere half of his true self."[2] That is, as well as the ultimate unity of God and man, there is the interim symbolic unity, found in "the mystical and positive meaning of the love between men and women."[3] Romantic love is not mere romanticism but a reflection of the transcendence of spiritual isolation. The second parallel is with a theme T. S.

Eliot used; he similarly put forward the idea of two ways to salvation: that of total self-dedication, extending to sainthood, and that of humble faithfulness, fulfilling with integrity the duties of ordinary life. These alternatives are outlined in several of Eliot's plays but are most explicit in *The Cocktail Party* and *The Confidential Clerk*.

The duke, of course, is thinking of increasing his own happiness, but this is only half the story. The true unity that exorcises loneliness requires commitment to the other person, even to the extent of feeling his or her pain, and his admitted refusal to care for the pain of others is, according to Rosabel, the duke's fatal flaw. His pain at Perpetua's apparently unexpected rejection of him is the catalyst to his recognition of other people's suffering. Though selfish pain need not lead to thought for the pain of others, in the duke's case, it fortunately does. The marriage to Rosabel, then, is not merely a piece of structural tidying up but represents the duke's conversion to what she represents: sympathy with suffering.

Perpetua, on the other hand, is striving to define herself, to detach herself from the "flocks of girls,"

> Inside or outside the prison, Perpetua
> (I thought), you're everybody's colour.
> You must make good before you break the bad,
> Perpetua.
>
> (1:179)

She is working toward true and responsible human freedom—the freedom to choose. Dominic's plan to marry her to the duke interferes with this achievement, cutting off again "my freedom of choice and my individual day" (1:182). The loss of her individual destiny makes her only a cipher, a representative of a general human lot, losing her unique human value, she feels, as she combs her hair in front of the observatory mirror in the Halloween ritual:

> And I am the eight duchesses
> And the three housekeepers and the chambermaid
> Combing their hair. I am any girl: Perpetua
> Perpetual, making no gesture I can call
> My own, engraving theirs one lifetime deeper.
>
> (1:213)

In Fry's scheme of things, this acquiescence in a repeated pattern is quite wrong for human beings. Humanity can learn of a universal divine purpose from the natural pattern of the rose, the thistle, the river weed, but as the plays repeatedly stress, humanity has no fixed pattern, and to try to become roselike or thistlelike is a degradation of the higher potential of humanity. That is why it is right for Perpetua to shake off the pressure on her freedom, just as Jennet was right to recoil from Humphrey's businesslike sex bargain:

> No, no, you're mistaken, and I was quite
> Mistaken, too! This isn't how I mean
> To lose my way, by force of circumstantial
> Evidence. When I lose my way I shall lose it
> In my own time, and by my own misguided
> Sense of direction.
>
> (1:216)

Perpetua already has the sympathy for others that the duke has to acquire, and although she resists the duke's emotional appeals briskly before rejecting him, she finds afterward that the problem of causing pain by her free, independent decisions affects her more deeply than Dominic's pragmatic coercion:

> No one is separate from another; how difficult
> That is. I move, and the movement goes from life
> To life all round me. And yet I have to be
> Myself. And what is *my* freedom becomes
> Another person's compulsion. What are we to make
> Of this dilemma?
>
> (1:244)

The question comes toward the end of the play, and the Perpetua theme does not answer this dilemma. Perpetua leaves the stage, rejecting firmly any further dalliance with the duke or with Edgar, and her future career is unknown. It is left to the duke to explain indirectly, beneath his almost self-parodying enthusiasm for the decay of nature, that acceptance of the amazing variety of life cannot have limitations and exceptions. His previous general appreciativeness had tried to exclude commitment and pain, but there must be an acceptance of the whole. This is presumably what Perpetua will have to accept too.

As in *Lady*, most of the characters surrounding the duke are strongly individualized, the least obtrusive being his son, Edgar—and this is Edgar's problem; he finds himself constantly eclipsed by his ebullient father. A transparently honest, generous young man, his impulse on realizing this problem is to bring it out into the open and avoid the sort of obsessiveness that preys on Rosabel: "For the first time in my young life / I'm jealous of my father. I thought I'd better / Mention it before I begin to brood" (1:194). He later bears no resentment toward Perpetua for having lied to conceal her assignation with his father, in spite of having obviously been hurt by this. His role is quite a small one in the plot, but thematically he reminds us of the younger generation to which the older must at last give way, and he shows both the duke's younger self and a more sensitive and responsible version of his colorful father.

Reedbeck and Dominic are apparently quite a different father and son pair. No doubt Dominic's moralizing, unforgiving self-righteousness is a reaction against his father's loquacious, affectionate dishonesty. Yet their characters and their subplot reflect the central theme. Reedbeck's bouncing cheerfulness, his decoration of neutral facts with excessive eloquence, and his imperviousness to the effect of his behavior on others parody similar qualities in his employer. However, he has no theory of maintaining detachment from the world; he displays an innocent enjoyment of his situation and refuses to follow up implications and consequences. "There's nothing unpleasant that isn't going to be pleasant" (1:155), he carols before Dominic starts threatening him. By his rhetoric he intensifies his enjoyment of life—as Jessie tells Perpetua, "Your father loves you / With every word in the language" (1:174)—and conceals from himself the basic dishonesty of his behavior:

> I hope
> I've done nothing so monosyllabic as to cheat.
> A spade is never so merely a spade as the word
> Spade would imply.
>
> (1:184)

But he accepts Perpetua's alternative: "What made you supercherify with chousery / The Duke?" (1:186). Instead of embezzlement, he refers to "a certain transposition; we might / Call this process Reedbequity" (1:185). Like the duke, Rosabel, and Hilda, he has a change of heart; he decides at last to confess and reform: "Now that my attention has been drawn / To what must be a myopia in my moral vision" (1:235).

Dominic, on the other hand, is an important instrument of the plot and illustrates the error of too much moral rigidity. He carries scruples to extremes and lacks the generosity that leavens Edgar's attitude. Later Fry was concerned that he had left him with a lesson seemingly unlearned at the end of the play. Dominic does recognize the folly of his interference in that Perpetua was in the dangerous burning house because he sent her there, but immediately he takes upon himself the right to suggest that Rosabel should expiate her fault by seeking punishment: "There's Sergeant Harry Bullen . . . I'm sure he'd arrest you / Willingly if you went and asked him" (1:226). The duke condemns this roundly when he finds out—"You think more of the sin than of the sinner" (1:241)—but Dominic's final line is ("with a sigh"), "Ethics are very difficult" (1:242).

Another grouping of contrasts is offered by the trio of former mistresses—Jessie, Hilda, and Rosabel. They are collectively compared to the goddesses Aphrodite, Hera, and Athene, among whom Paris had to judge, and the duke specifies that Hilda is Athene. Hilda has the wisdom to analyze and try to come to terms with the disturbing revival of the past, and she reinforces Rosabel's point that the duke's invitation has been issued without thought for the feelings of the guests:

> I know him painstakingly enough
> To be sure it was kindly meant; it couldn't have been
> To watch our faces fall . . . There
> Was still something in me to be hurt,
> Which a little surprised me.
>
> (1:192–93)

She is wise enough, though, not to become obsessed by the problem. She is another person who finds a lower but still virtuous path to salvation, in reconciling herself with her husband, Roderic, the "height of depth" (1:193), his mind a "flat horizon" (1:194) peopled by "a few sheep-like thoughts" (1:193). She feels a shock of reawakened sympathy, such as Perpetua feels for the rejected duke or the duke himself feels for the imprisoned Rosabel, because of a sudden access of misfortune and suffering, though in Roderic's case, it is appropriately physical, not mental, torment. Hilda explains later:

> Two ribs broken, and a slight concussion,
> Nothing worse. But that was enough to show me
> How bad it is to see Roderic hurt, but how
> Intolerable it would be to see Roderic
> Maimed, or dying day by day; and I sat
> Beside him and marvelled, and wondered how
> So much could lie there in a human shell,
> The long succession of life that led to him,

> Uninterrupted from the time
> Of time's aching infancy.
>
> (1:240)

Jessie, on the other hand, is Hera, the queen goddess, large in size and heart, perhaps even more of an earth mother than a queen. Fry said of her, "She is nearest to the placid accepting animal" ("Venus Considered," 5), which the duke recognizes when arguing that his first act gathering, like all humanity, is essentially alone: "We shall all feel quite alone, except, perhaps, Jessie" (1:162). During the play, she does not develop or need to develop; her response to Hilda's questioning is only, "I like being here / So much I never even wondered" (1:192). She speaks for the natural currents in human life, and her advice is, "Let them be, because be they will" (1:193), "If you think you can, then do" (1:196), and "When someone knocks you down, it doesn't improve things to knock yourself up" (1:204).

Then, as the thematic structure shows, Rosabel, the Aphrodite figure who eventually wins the contest, has the function of making the duke feel for others' suffering, but as a character, she is rather shadowily established. When Fry later blamed his digression into translating Anouilh's *L'Invitation au château* for having had a bad effect on his interrupted composition of *Venus*—"I have always promised myself that if I live long enough I will revise it nearer to my liking"—it was the character of Rosabel he had in mind.[4] Her entrance is effectively anticlimactic; she arrives during Dominic's confrontation with Reedbeck and is totally bewildered by their distraught behavior and non sequiturs. She concludes in a little aside:

> I begin to understand why the theatre
> Gives me so little work.
> That could scarcely have been called a splendid entrance,
> Even by the most loving.
>
> (1:158)

And when she bursts into her offended condemnation of his behavior, she makes a considerable impression, but in between she has not been given the opportunity to build up her effect on the audience as fully human rather than merely neurotic. Edgar gives her the apple first, so she must have struck him as the most charming, but at this stage, the actress has to make this impression by acting between her very sparse lines. In acts 2 and 3, Rosabel has a nervous, brooding, hunted sort of dialogue, with short, abrupt questions and exclamations, and perhaps an even more histrionic turn of phrase than most of the others, suitable to her theatrical background. In her despairing confession to Dominic she cries:

> You're mad! Do you think I hurled myself away
> From all the decent world for your sake?
> Hate me, hate me! Oh, why is it
> You won't understand?
>
>   (1:226)

But she prepares to meet the village policeman with an engaging return of her original anxiety for her image: "But now I shall give myself up. Do I look / Plain and frightful? It could scarcely matter / Less" (1:227). Some kind of little scene or a few speeches about her life, disappointments, and hopes between her affair with the duke and the present would round her character further.

The two comic servants, Reddleman and Bates, are necessary in that the setting Fry has chosen has to have servants. They are not merely more colorful versions of the silent maids and footmen of other comedies of high life; rather, both reflect the main theme by managing through concern for others to overcome faults of character,—in Reddleman's case, his loss of nerve as a former lion tamer, and for Bates, the stigma of his past burglaries. Both put themselves in danger to rescue the duke and Perpetua. Apart from this, their mutual hostility and their idiosyncratic language—Reddleman's Irish verbosity and Bates's cockney malapropisms—add to the comedy.

Fry thought first of the atmosphere and outline of the play, and more than in most of his plays since *A Boy with a Cart*, there is a sense of the characters being figures in a landscape. The autumnal atmosphere generates many of the unifying images, though, strictly speaking, several relate to decline without being specifically connected with autumn. The eclipse, for instance, another major symbol, could happen at any season; the decay of the duke's house is, as Hilda points out, unnecessarily pronounced for a mansion with an evidently well-to-do owner:

> It looks as though the walls have cried themselves
> To sleep for nights on end. And the number of windows
> Broken! I don't think you should throw nearly
> So many stones. The spiders are larger, the jackdaws
> Ruder, the servants more eccentric. You mustn't

> Drift into Gothic, when your physique is so
> Stubbornly Norman.
>
> (1:164)

The neglect is intentional: the duke admits that he is making its more enduring architecture reflect his own "deft and reckless plunge into ancient history"
(1:164). Autumn is one of the many images of natural decay, from the single
diurnal cycle—"I have to consider my years and decline with the sun"
(1:160)—to the crumbling of the solidest bricks and mortar. The key word is
natural and implies "inevitable," as the duke seems to accept in his own assumption of autumnal imagery: "For years the frost has lain / On my stub-
ble beard. The swallows and other such / Migratory birds have left me
months ago" (1:159). The delusion of perpetual youth suggested by
Perpetua's arrival is thus shown from the first to be contrary to natural
progression.

The parallel theme of the duke's detachment from his surroundings is related to the constellations he observes, less subject to measurable decay than
the sublunary world of nature, and where distance lends beauty to the view.
He considers that the pleasure of beauty depends on seeing it from afar. As
the stars have a distant beauty, so humanity has an impersonal beauty at the
same distance:

> Here we're as dull as unwashed plates; out there
> We shine. That's a consideration. Come
> Close to paradise, and where's the lustre?
> But still, at some remove, we shine, and truth
> We hope is content to keep a distant prospect . . .
> . . . To take us separately is to stare
> At mud; only together, at long range,
> We coalesce in light.
>
> (1:168)

Here the "together" refers only to humanity as an interesting range of phe-
nomena from which the duke himself remains detached, not to his own
unity with other human beings. The individual remains alone ("except,
perhaps, Jessie"), and Saturn and its rings, which he shows Perpetua in the
observatory scene, is an image of relentless solitude: "You see them there, /
You see how they circle and never touch. / Saturn is alone, for all their circling round him" (1:208).

The natural world, particularly the English landscape, insinuates its lesson to humanity. The duke has noticed that "all the world's life" (1:201)—the patient toad, the indolent fish, the waving weed—has a being and necessity denied to human beings, and his eventual acceptance of his different human destiny is also seen in natural imagery:

> The realm of bryony, sloes, rose-hips,
> And a hedge's ruin, a golden desuetude,
> A countryside like a drowned angel
> Lying in shallow water, every thorn
> Tendering a tear.
>
> (1:246)

Although he at first disparaged "this draughty time" with its "slipshod leaves, / Leaves disbanded, leaves at a loose end" (1:170), the autumnal imagery is mostly Keatsian in its suggestions of plenty, richness, color, and beauty. Interestingly, there is no suggestion of cyclical progression to rebirth in this natural image—nor does the duke draw even a fallacious encouragement from the sun's recovery from eclipse.

But there are other important symbols, particularly the fire at the center of the play. Rosabel confusedly mentions Nero's Rome in her plans, but the point about that myth is that Nero was said to have fiddled while Rome burned, in an ultimate display of irresponsibility, while Rosabel hopes her fire will have the opposite effect on the duke. This fire is much more integrated as a symbol than the burning of *Lady*, which was simply the threat of death in a particularly painful form—beheading or hanging would have been almost as functional there. Here, not only does the threat of death frighten Perpetua into the duke's arms in a last instinctive grasping after life, as any other such threat would do, but it also symbolizes the misplaced passions of the duke. Fire is a traditional romantic symbol for uncontrolled passion, and in the next act, the fire is reflected in the lake in drizzling rain, an obvious sign of the extinction of the duke's passion and hopes. On a smaller scale, Perpetua's unresponsiveness to his feeling appears on two separate occasions when he asks her, "Matches?" and she replies laconically, "No" (1:207, 231).

Another set of symbols includes the pistol and the apple. The award of the apple has been whimsically organized by the duke, and Perpetua, though not in the secret, responds intuitively to its symbolic aspect—"it appeared to be, in a misty way, / Like a threat to my new-come freedom" (1:179). With her pistol, she destroys this threat and asserts her freedom. An apple then reappears in the Halloween ritual, itself suggesting entrapment in an eternal stereotype: "Perpetua / Perpetual, making no gesture I can call / My own, engraving theirs one lifetime deeper" (1:213). The duke still sees the apple as representing the success of his schemes, for he escapes through the flames with the apple in his teeth.

The archery visually represents the competition of the duke and Edgar; the duke is a Sagittarian, Rosabel tells us (1:160), and as well as the references to Cupid's bow, arrows, like pistols, are well-known phallic symbols. If Perpetua was asserting an unconventionally virile independence with her pistol, Edgar is marking a more traditional supercession of his father by his arrow, which goes "nearer the gold than his" (1:196). Bullet and arrow both predict the failure of the duke's plans.

Verbally, though not visually, a theme of imprisonment runs through the play, the reverse of the free choice Perpetua is striving for. She has been in prison in America and faces marriage with the duke as the prospect of life-long metaphorical imprisonment to save Reedback literally from prison in his turn: "If someone has to go to prison, / I must," losing "my freedom of choice and my individual day," with "Broad Cupid's arrows on my wedding veil" (1:182); her enticing smile "will be like the glint of handcuffs" (1:184). Finally Rosabel commits herself to prison to expiate her arson, after which, for her, marriage to the duke and freedom will coincide.

There is a strong symbolic support running through the plot, and, unlike the crucifixion in *Thor* and the sharing of bread and wine in *Phoenix*, already provided by the initial underlying allegory, Fry is inventing new symbols as he develops his original story. The imagery in the language is as plentiful as in *Phoenix* and *Lady*, though the language seems to have changed register and become more formal in spite of the modern setting. (Peter Brook commented, "Although *Venus Observed* is in modern clothes, it is hardly a contemporary play.")[5]

Most of the characters freely play with classical, biblical, and historical allusions with a familiarity that is not contemporary. Perpetua invites Reedback: "Come and judge what a huntress I should make, / What a rival for Artemis, and what chance Actaeon / Would have if I pursued him" (1:188–89). Her complex syntax is as formal as her references. She muses on the duke's exposition of Saturn's solitary orbit:

> I'm looking at the same star
> That shone alone in the wake of Noah's
> Drifting ark as soon as the rain was over,
> That shone on shining Charlemagne

> Far away, and as clear
> As the note of Roland's homing horn . . .
>
> (1:208)

Like her less allusive but carefully poetical characterization of her native land—

> If this is still an island
> Enclosed in a druid circle of stony sea,
> As misty as it was that chilly Thursday
> When I was born to the wilting of plovers
> And the smell of a saturation of hops,
> Then I'm safely and happily home.
>
> (1:176)

—Perpetua's language is carefully organized and full of imagery. Highly articulate dialogue of various kinds—poetic, rhetorical, polysyllabic—used in a comedy is constantly confronted by unheroic situations and ideas for the sake of comic contrast, and the serious use of poetry treads a thin line between beauty and bathos. In these examples, Perpetua remains on the windy side of beauty, though there may be a kind of self-consciousness to it, a sense of using unusual words—but insisting on their beauty nevertheless.

Characteristic of Fry's method is Perpetua's self-mocking speech in the observatory when, accused of stemming a potential tide of love by her laconic replies, she embarks on a sentence forty-four lines long, which is obviously a performance, first for the duke and then for the audience: "There isn't any reason / Why a sentence, I suppose, once it begins . . . shouldn't go / Endlessly moving" (1:210). It is language as display, not trying to deceive but appealing for appreciation on its own terms. And in among the "forgetful music / Looping and threading, tuning and entwining" (1:210), Perpetua interweaves the typical imagery of music, bells, the harmony of the "muted spheres" (1:211), the rivers and seas of the "oath intoning-ocean" (1:210), which has appeared in *Phoenix* and *Lady*.

The duke has some of the most Shakespearean of speeches—for instance, in describing archery or the witching hour on Halloween, an impression prompted by subject matter to some extent but also by the thoughtful creation of a scene by verbal associations, as well as tactile images:

> All-Hallows Eve. If the earth is ever wise
> To magic, this is the night when magic's wisdom
> Comes rolling in across our sedate equation.

> All the closed hours unlock; the rigorous ground
> Grows as soft as the sea, exhaling
> The bloom of the dead everywhere. They almost
> Live again: as nearly, at least, as we
> Can brush on death. And through the night
> They trespass agreeably on our time of trespasses,
> Molesting the air in a pale, disinterested
> Way . . .
>
> (1:212)

The temptation to label the autumnal descriptions Keatsean results not only from the analogy of subject but from a sensuousness that runs through the rest of the play. Some of the most memorable speeches are lists that make their effect by visual, aural, or tactile associations, as in Edgar's offer:

> The cloudy peach, the bristling pineapple,
> The dropsical pear, the sportive orange,
> Apricot, sloe, King William, or a carillon
> Of grapes . . .
>
> (1:177)

In Perpetua's list of autumn colors, the melancholy effect depends on the choice of associative noun:

> Lemon, amber,
> Umber, bronze and brass, oxblood, damson,
> Crimson, scalding scarlet, black cedar
> And the willow's yellow fall to grace.
>
> (1:182)

As every advertiser knows, the impact would be quite different if the same colors had been labeled "primrose, marmalade, . . ." and so on.

On the other hand, often Fry exaggerates contrasting speech styles, including the heroic and poetic, to exploit their comic incongruity. A simple example is the change from demanding epithets and classical names—

> If Paris had no trouble
> Choosing between the tide-turning beauty,
> Imponderable and sexed with eternity,
> Of Aphrodite, Hera, and Athene . . .

—to the colloquial expression and familiar names of the rest of the same sentence:

> . . . Aren't you ashamed to make heavy weather of a choice
> Between Hilda, and Rosabel, and Jessie?
>
> (1:150)

In a more spectacular example, when Perpetua asks whether the floor is swaying, the duke replies:

> The floor is battering at your feet like Attila
> With a horde of corybantic atoms,
> And travelling at eighteen miles a second,
> But it cannot be said to sway.
>
> (1:175)

Fry is not using the extravagance of language simply for comic effect; it also illustrates the duke's determined refusal to be concerned by anything, microcosmic or macrocosmic, that faces him, and simultaneously it reminds us of the constant theme of wonder: here, that both mythic choices and the laws of physics coexist with the ordinary routine of life.

Some of the metaphoric embellishment of the dialogue is questioned and thus acknowledged as exceptional, as when Reedbeck tries to change the subject during Rosabel's outburst: "It would be fanciful / No doubt to say that the moon has placed a penny / Not on the dead but on the living eye of the sun," and Edgar represses him with, "Yes, Reedbeck, it would" (1:169). Usually, however, the expression of meaning through metaphor goes without comment. "The mouth of the moon has begun to munch," says the duke, introducing the eclipse. "We shall all feel ourselves making a north-west passage / Through the sea of heaven . . ." (1:151). And even in more desperate straits, Perpetua finds brief but original metaphors: "I can hear the flames / Crunching on wood . . . the garden's / Capering with light" (1:218).

A new and significant development in Fry's versification that is added to the texture of the verse without anything being taken away is the increased attention to the effect of line endings. Fry had defensively said of *Lady* that the poetry was a continuous medium and its lineation was unimportant, but he admitted privately that he would later have preferred to move some of the line divisions to make more impact. In *Venus* this has been attended to. Sentences run smoothly on, but in some places, the tiny possible pause at the ends of lines has rhetorical emphasis. It is seen particularly in the speeches of

Reedbeck—for instance, where the greater emphasis on the second *poor* clearly comes from its positioning:

> Poor little girl, poor
> Little girl.
>   (1:190)

The duke's half-formal, half-playful speech exploits this too:

> A good father must be a man. And what
> Is a man? Edgar, what is a man? O
> My man-child, what in the world is a man?
>   (1:200)

The verse is giving guidance to the actor—and reader—as to the emphasis and phrasing of the lines. There is, in fact, more evidence that Fry was concerned with indicating tone and stress in the dialogue in this play. There are a few more stage directions, particularly of manner "abstractedly . . . glumly . . . in a sudden burst of rage," and rather more italics: "Good gracious, a *sound* like a shot!" (1:177), and "Oh *I* should have been; / It would have seemed like a thunder clap to *me*" (1:189). And Reedbeck's haste in trying to prevent or detect Dominic's incriminating him to Perpetua naturally results in breathlessness, which is specified in the stage direction as well as shown in a speech broken by punctuation, repetition, and line breaks:

> So here—here—
> You are. I wondered, missed you, but luckily caught
> Sight of you going down through the trees. I lost
> My hat on the way; it blew (oh, what a gasping old fellow)
> Off, blew off . . .
>   (1:183)

This is humorous in the would-be casual small talk and guilty anxiety betrayed by the uncasual haste of arrival, and as in the earlier plays, though much of the humor seems to be verbal, its full force often comes from the simultaneous effect of words and action. Like the duke, Reedbeck is consciously eloquent, clear in his use of language to conceal the criminality of his "Reedbequity." He has an imaginative repertoire of insulting epithets, a great resource of comedy. Paradoxically he laments his limitations in the midst of inventiveness:

You're a vain, vexing, incomprehensible.
Crimping, constipated duffer. What's your heart?
All plum duff! Why do I have to be
So inarticulate? God give me a few
Lithontriptical words! You grovelling little
Gobemouche! . . .
. . . You spigoted, bigoted, operculated prig!
(1:190)

Part of the effect here comes from Reedbeck's physically shaking Dominic
while he says all this and then dropping him sprawling on the ground. This is
followed by an example of the incongruity of words and situation exploited
in *Lady*. Jessie's polite "How do you do? Please don't bother to get up"
(1:190) is the sort of phrase usually addressed to gentlemen seated in more
formal and correct circumstances, and her soothing, "It was lovely exercise for
both of you," again is magnificently inadequate to the rage and violence that
accompanied the vigorous movements. On another level, many of Jessie's
conscious or unconsciously comic remarks conceal a deeper truth. The running joke of the second act, when the other characters in turn interrupt her
letter writing with their problems, partly depends on the fact that she is writing "to my father, eighty-seven. He can't read a word / Of my handwriting,
and doesn't try, but he likes / The postman" (1:191). When the duke asks,
"if he'll never read it, do you have to write so much?" she replies, "Well, no,
but he lives such a long way out of the village / I like to make it worth the
postman's while" (1:204). Under this illogical argument is a different logic:
Jessie is putting in an absolute amount of care and effort as a tribute to the
postman's effort and in a way is at one with that human effort.

The balance of comedy and seriousness is more equally effected here than
in the earlier plays. One critic noted shrewdly that "this play cuts much
deeper into human feeling than his earlier work."[6] This comment may under-
estimate *Lady* but does justice to the theme of sympathy and suffering that
underlies the plot. Most of the main characters are allowed speeches of serious
self-revelation, as in Rosabel's initial anger and later remorse, Hilda's self-
analysis, and the duke's various examinations of his "ego agonistes" (1:217).

The duke's and Perpetua's response to the fire is more fully established
than Jennet's to her prospective burning. Where Jennet's obvious fear kept
being submerged in the comic action, the immediate crisis of the observatory
fire allows due concentration on its effect on the characters. Perpetua panics in
an entirely understandable way, and Fry recognizes that realistic brevity con-
veys the essential truth of the situation better than more eloquent poetry:

"No! No, no! / Not that way!," she cries. "Please, / Please, please, please" (1:218), and replies to the duke's poetic attempts to seek refuge in love with "I'm afraid of the fire, I'm afraid, I am so / Afraid of the fire" (1:221). Simple instinctive fear has blotted out other considerations, and its expression needs hardly more than a cry of anguish. Like the fragile moth, noticed earlier in the scene, she beats herself uselessly against the window in terror. The duke is brave and collected but not frivolous, and he tries to coax Perpetua to risk the collapsing staircase with repeated and patient resistance to her fears; again, he does not make light of a serious predicament. And although Perpetua is frightened into helplessness in the fire, she afterward shows the moral courage to rescind her declaration of love and reaffirm her more deliberate choice, in another moment of pain.

The coexistence of comic and tragic works well in the text, without uneasy dilution of the effects of one by the other, though Olivier told Fry afterward that the fire scene seemed in production to peter out in a mixture of styles and moods; the lunatic conclusion did not seem to produce the punch the audience was expecting. The farce of the rescuers' wrangling over the victims may need taking up more boldly where Olivier was trying to avoid it. The play was written for Laurence Olivier, who was launching his own management at the St. James's Theatre and wanted a Fry play for his opening production, and he both starred and directed. This first production was very popular with audiences but not entirely successful in presenting its unified message.

Critics were more reconciled to Fry's style, but there were still demands for more plot and more story, and there was some bafflement as to the meaning. T. C. Worsley queried both the style—as acceptable but operating under a law of diminishing returns—and the impact on stage, in that the judgment of Paris theme "as actually handled was simply thrown away. The entrances of each of the three mistresses were thoroughly ill-contrived." He also had the impression that the play gave "the minimum of opportunity to the actors. Sir Laurence Olivier as the duke has a part that calls for nothing but an easy command and a negligent air. Sir Laurence supplies them both of course."[7] W. A. Wilcox, finding some deficiencies, blamed the text for them: "Olivier stumbled twice in a lengthy declamation, and looked blankly at his audience, who looked just as blankly back."[8] And Harold Hobson cruelly added that "some, but not all, of the other acting recalled that of a really good girls' school."[9]

Only one or two critics looked beyond the plot mechanism to note the underlying moral problem—that the duke "makes witty, philosophic, generous words do the work of a heart"—and nobody commented that the declamations, lengthy or otherwise, are giving the philosophy behind the moral changes that take place in almost every character in the play.[10] On the other hand, the critics' mutual contradictions and unsupported views here, as elsewhere, make the value of reviews questionable. Hobson, for instance, has a burst of rage about "the fireplace that Roger Furse has put in the middle of the fourth wall of the Duke of Altair's observatory. This is no doubt a concession to those realists who demand that the fourth wall shall be piled high with furniture even if the audience is thereby prevented from seeing what happens on the stage."[11] It sounds as though the front of the stage was obstructed by a colossal chimneypiece, but stage photographs show little more than an unobtrusive pair of ankle-high fire irons.

The set as a whole appears in photographs as neat, elegant, and ducal, as do the costumes and cast, and Fry commented afterward of this production, comparing it with Gielgud's *Lady*: "Well, again, in many ways—and I think it's largely my own fault in the writing—this happened; the realities get a bit lost in the surface entertainment and the comedy perhaps. . . . It may be simply that the style of the play is misleading. I'd thought of it very much more as happening in a strange, crumbling world, an autumnal world, where life is being lived in the knowledge of death, and it was not quite like that in the production, or in the writing either."[12]

When *Venus* was done in America, Laurence Olivier directed it, with Rex Harrison playing the duke and Lili Palmer as Perpetua, and he ensured that the set was much more crumbling and fusty. Nonetheless, Olivier argued that many compromises had to be made for the sake of acceptability to the audience and the powers of the cast.[13] The Rosabel problem, for instance, he said, was that she was underwritten and needed a big star to enact all that was missing in such a small part—which a big star would not be interested in doing. On the other hand, Fry had always wanted Perpetua's set-piece "sentence" in their love scene played without movement or business, perfectly still, and Olivier directed this way in New York and found it worked admirably. But he decided that it would be impossibly self-conscious to have the duke's Halloween speech also spoken without movement, as Fry would have liked.

The principle of giving a free hand to the director comes into conflict with the playwright's feeling that the play should include his original vision—a vision that dramatists such as Shaw would firmly impose by detailed and evocative stage directions. Writing for a major actor may also inevitably result in the subordination of the play to its star, a problem Fry was to plunge into again.

Chapter Seven

Problems of Perfection:
The Dark Is Light Enough

The Dark Is Light Enough appeared after *A Sleep of Prisoners,* but I have opted to discuss it here alongside the two preceding seasonal comedies to show how it furthers Fry's development of the comic form. It was written especially for Edith Evans and produced in 1954, and Fry is attempting to show at length the difficult subject of goodness in action. The traditional justification of comedy is its corrective function; vice, folly, affectation, and deviation are ridiculed and rejected, essentially a negative process. This is what we see in the satirical presentation of the selfish townsfolk of Cool Clary and the isolationism of the duke of Altair. In *The Dark Is Light Enough,* however, amid the gross errors of certain characters, Countess Rosmarin Ostenburg exemplifies goodness, without any of the blunders or waverings apparent in Jennet or Perpetua. The problem here is the audience's resistance toward the perfect character, and Fry seeks to avoid this by giving the countess a conscious sense of humor and an unconscious amusing naiveté, as well as exploiting the other onstage characters' resistance to, or at least their exasperation with, her inconvenient unworldliness. Edith Evans, the first countess, was known for her charm and magnetism, and she charmed her way out of priggishness with great success, though some critics felt that her personal charisma obscured the underlying values of the play.

The plot unfolds according to Fry's favored pattern, with a first act gradually bringing all the characters onstage and building up to a crisis involving most of the cast. Initially only three of the usual guests of Countess Rosmarin's Thursday evening salon are present, which is not surprising as there is both a snowstorm and an approaching army of Hungarian revolutionaries to deter visitors. The guests, all old friends, are Jakob, Belmann, and Dr. Kassel, and they remain onstage throughout the act as an explanatory and exclamatory chorus. First they establish for each other and the audience their concern that the countess seems to be absent for the first Thursday for twenty years, having apparently harnessed two horses to the great sleigh and driven out into danger and blizzard. The countess's house is close to

Vienna, just on the Austrian side of the Austro-Hungarian border, and her young son, Stefan, who wanders in and out in a state of anxiety, has sent to Vienna for her daughter, Gelda, and son-in-law, Count Peter Zichy.

About a third of the act is given to this exposition, which includes a digression on the character of one Richard Gettner and his earlier marriage to Gelda, now annulled. Then the fairly low-key atmosphere of the humorous sparring among the three friends is suddenly raised by the appearance of Gettner in the first of three dramatic entrances from above that introduce a complete change of tone. This is one of Fry's highly theatrical effects; the difference of stage levels is exploited in that the other characters are absorbed in the simultaneous arrival of Gelda and do not see Gettner's appearance above and his slow descent of the stairs, while the audience's attention is immediately attracted by this high and dominant entrance, and then suspense is built up in waiting for the other characters to react.

We have heard from Belmann, who obviously had never liked him, that Gettner had once written a brilliant book and then lapsed into being a drunken idler, "a pest / Who never left us, and never loved us" (3:71), and had recently and unpredictably joined the Hungarian revolutionary army. He proceeds to live up to Belmann's savage characterization in provoking by word or tone most of those who speak to him. If Gettner's entry has been delayed, the countess's is more so, and her friends and family, having built up audience expectation by their discussion of her, now swarm around her with concern and excitement, distracting attention from Gettner until she refers to him ominously as "poor hunted Richard" (3:81). Gettner recaptures the limelight briskly: "I'm a deserter, simply, I expect / You understand that" (3:81). The argument about the dangers of harboring a deserter goes on at some length, allowing Gettner to demonstrate further his unpleasantness and the hostility of Stefan and the others. To the countess, the rescue is too simple a matter to argue about, and it is left to Gelda to voice the more charitable view for her. Once the issues have been laid out, the situation is moved to a higher level of suspense by the arrival of the Hungarian troops at the gates. Gettner is bundled off into the belfry to hide, as Colonel Janik, a Hungarian officer, already known to the countess and her circle as an amateur geologist, comes in and asks for the fugitive.

The countess's behavior at once shows true goodness and yet is difficult for an audience to accept. She does not lie to the colonel to protect Gettner; she simply refuses to give him up and seeks to persuade the colonel not to pursue him. The fact that lying would not have done any good because Gettner had been seen arriving is immaterial; she did not know this and is refusing on principle to compromise or make the ends justify the means. Now Fry adds his usual second turn of the screw as Janik produces her son-in-law, Count Peter, captured and hostage, offered in exchange for Gettner. And the countess refuses again. Count Peter is not in fact being threatened with instant death, merely continued captivity of a not very safe kind, and he is an honorable man who does not wish to buy his life at the expense of another, so the situation is not on a tragic level. Nevertheless, the other characters burst into the discussion with indignation. The countess is adamant, and, as in *Lady*, the act ends on a note of anxiety and unresolved crisis.

The second act moves the action and the countess's household out into the superior stables, while the Hungarians, who have marched on into an unexpected fight with a party of Austrians, take over the house for their wounded. This act develops two minor subplots, involving Gettner and the countess's children, who come out to talk to him in his new hiding place in a loft above the stables. Stefan briefly seeks to understand Gettner's motives, and suggests the test of a duel with himself, which he refuses.

Gelda's reassurances develop in the opposite way into an intimate scene during which she seeks to reassess her past feelings for Gettner in their short marriage and thereby reawakens what she calls "a feeling of no definition" that nevertheless brings dangerously powerful tenderness and susceptibility, and they kiss. These preliminaries are a preparation for Gettner's further attack on his protector's tolerance. In the meantime the action becomes full of movement and variety: Gettner hides; soldiers come in and out carrying furniture; the countess arrives with Colonel Janik; Jakob and Belmann bicker as usual, observed by Stefan. Even Count Peter is allowed to join the party with his guards, and the countess remarks, "I seem almost to be undoing / The events of yesterday" (3:118). Gettner, however, in his role as troublemaker, cannot allow this. In another dramatic entry from above, slowly and insecurely descending the ladder, too drunk to remember his previous desperation for life, he leaves his hiding place. The audience sees him, then one by one the horrified guests notice him, and all wait in suspense for the guards, last of all, to catch sight of their quarry.

This act consists of a series of lurches toward disaster. Deceptively the countess manages once more to draw back from the brink by charming the guards into ignoring Gettner, but her reward is the serious blow of seeing Gettner advance his provocative claims on Gelda and kiss her again before Count Peter's face. The countess's generous action seems to have led to damage to her daughter's happy marriage, and she is deeply disturbed, though she does not denounce Gettner, but forcibly redirects the mood of the gathering by getting the guards to dance and sing. Neither she nor the other characters notice that Stefan is forcing a quarrel on the drunken Gettner. There is

enough byplay as the countess seeks to learn an improper song from the soldiers for the audience to forget Gettner and to share the characters' shock
when the singing is abruptly broken by pistol shots. This is the climax of tension toward which the action has been tending. Gettner appears, distraught
and incoherent, and again in this ultimate trial of her generosity, the countess
does not blame him: "All I am asking, Richard, / Is the courage of an answer.
Not why; / But whether I go on without him" (3:137). Her attempts to
dominate his confusion and find out the worst increase suspense until Dr.
Kassel comes to say Stefan is wounded but alive. Even now, the countess tries
to shield Gettner from the angry reactions of the guards, but he is still unre-
sponsive to her generosity, and the act ends unresolved as the countess gathers
her obviously failing strength to go to her son.

More happens between the acts in *Dark* than in the earlier plays. Act 3
opens some days later; it is Thursday again, Gettner has escaped on horse-
back, and the Hungarians have departed, fought a major battle with the
Austrians, and been definitively defeated. The opening of the act echoes that
of act 2, with a brief appearance of Stefan, now recovering, followed by a
scene of explanation between Gelda and her husband, who has been freed.
She has realized that "you and I are the truth" (3:145) and has rejected the
less controllable feeling that followed her excusable concern for Gettner. This
episode balances the one with Gettner and concludes Gelda's positive role in
the plot. As Count Peter hurries off to Vienna to try to stop the savage Austrian reprisals against the Hungarian prisoners, the action widens to include
the usual chorus of Belmann, Jakob, and Kassel. The doctor is telling the
others that the countess's illness is so serious that she is unlikely to live more
than a day or two, when Rosmarin herself is seen descending the staircase in
the last of the dramatic entries from above. Here the audience shares the characters' breathless anxiety as to whether the countess, stubbornly independent
as usual, can succeed in making her dying body obey her dominant will.

As Gelda had predicted, the countess has accepted the nearness of death
and is explaining the advantages of the finite life when a further surprise is
sprung on the household: a tap at the window heralds the entrance of a
bedraggled and fugitive Colonel Janik. He has come in despair to confront
Count Peter with the brutality of the Austrian government, but the countess restrains and draws him back to a sense of life by insisting that he remind
her of the soldiers' improper marching song, and while he is off balance, she
proposes to hide and save him—to the dismay of her friends. No sooner has
he gone into hiding than yet another surprise is produced: Richard Gettner
reappears, his escape interrupted by the countrywide rumors of the
countess's death.

Here the plot and situation seem more entangled than ever, especially to her exasperated friends, but this peak of turmoil and confusion is ruthlessly diminished by the countess, who insists on being alone with Gettner. The earlier comedies also end with a quiet sequence between two characters, but where *Lady* and *Venus* ended with peaceful statements of reconciliation, *Dark* still has some conflict to develop. First Gettner, though offended to hear that his enemy, Janik, is ensconced in "his" hiding place, proposes marriage to the countess. He assumes that her protection of him, and indeed her earlier arrangement of his marriage, must be signs of love. Gently but truthfully she convinces him that not only has she not loved him but she "could like you no more than occasionally" (3:164). He leaves in disgust. This seems like a failure of all Rosmarin's efforts during the play, but suddenly Gettner reappears, explaining that the Austrians, Janik's pursuers, are at the door. But the countess is dead. And at last, instead of escaping by the back way, Gettner decides to stay and confront the Austrians, exposing his own life to save his enemy.

The complications and reversals of this plot meant that critics of the first production had to agree that the play offered more action and fewer words than its predecessors. There was still confusion about its meaning, however, although some critics perceived the message beneath the action-packed events. Caryl Brahms said, "Mr. Fry has summoned us to consider not the perils of Hide and Seek played in the attic in a revolution, but a state of mind. We might call it Enlightenment."[1] The motif of the soldier and the lady, which appeared in *Phoenix, Lady,* and perhaps also in vestigial form in *The Firstborn* and *Thor,* represented something different every time. Here the lady is the more powerful figure, but she represents and seems explicitly to advocate pacifism, though Fry did not intend her to be immutable on this principle.[2] She also believes in both passive resistance to what she considers wrong and nonviolent pressure to persuade others of her own philosophy. Only if we recognize these elements of her pacifism can we understand the place of Gettner, who does not need persuading to be unmilitary, as Colonel Janik does; nor is he a deserter who needs to be persuaded back to militarism. What he must achieve is the difficult courage to pursue the right without physical defenses.

These two main characters have to bear the symbolic significance of the action. The role of the countess is signaled initially by Belmann:

> You know the Countess has the qualities of true divinity.
> For instance: how apparently undemandingly
> She moves among us; and yet

> Lives make and unmake themselves in her neighbourhood
> As nowhere else.
>
> (3:68–69)

Certainly she is seen to apply a certain amount of influence to make others do as she wishes. Persuading Janik to abandon his pursuit of Gettner, she argues that her house has provided shelter for the wounded Hungarians only because they were led there by Gettner, who therefore ought to be pardoned his desertion: "Desertion, / As you generously admit, has now / Changed into benefit" (3:117). Later she counters Janik's self-deprecatory despair "I've troubled this house enough"—with, "Then you won't want to put me to the trouble / Of persuading you, but simply hide yourself" (3:155). At other points, however, she leaves her friends to the responsibility of their own moral decisions. For instance, she does not reproach or admonish Gettner or Gelda. Her influence is in positive directions, but she makes no repressive, preventive, or punitive moves; her friends are free to reject her persuasions. In all these ways, she has "the qualities of true divinity" in loving and hoping for the betterment of humanity while leaving that development entirely to human free will. Gettner is wrong at the end of the play when he complains, "You never showed / Any expectations of me when you were alive, / Why should you now?" (3:166). *Expectation* is a word that recurs in the text. Gettner explains his early fascination with the countess's confident "stability" in those terms: "I was half caught in an expectation of life / Which she was good enough to show no sign / Of expecting from me" (3:108). And he then rejects the role of "disappointer of expectations" (3:109), only to recur to it bitterly in his drunken state: "Never come up to expectations, / They'll expect again and quite differently" (3:129). Gettner plays the role of Everyman to the countess's divinity, an Everyman who is prevented from lapsing into animal torpor by the tacit, unnerving sense of God's expectations. As Cain protests in *A Sleep of Prisoners*, the possibility of animal contentment is ruined by the silent pressure to achieve some higher state.

In the context of the blind movement upward and onward of the whole of humanity, each individual has an unique part to play: the whole is important, and the individual is equally important. This is why the countess is concerned for Richard Gettner, who as an individual soul is as important as any other saint or sinner:

> Life has a hope of him
> Or he would never have lived. Colonel,
> Can you prophesy the outcome of your war?

> Yet you still go about it. Richard lives
> In his own right, Colonel, not in yours
> Or mine.
>
> (3:118)

Both unique and representative, Gettner ultimately means to the countess "simply what any life may mean" (3:164). He has free will, which he uses ingloriously in saving his life, out of the instinct of self-preservation. The countess preserves him so that his particular destiny can work itself out, so that he has a longer reprieve of time in which freely to reach the human betterment God longs for. The countess's family and friends think little of the chances of his improving in any way. Even Gelda comments, "What help can there ever be for Richard?" (3:83). When the colonel poses the choice between Gettner and Count Peter, the others see no hope for the former:

> KASSEL: Still, if I thought that you wanted another opinion,
> Rosmarin, I should give my opinion against you.
>
> BELMANN: Philosophically, Countess, you may be reasonable,
> But humanly I see no point of balance
> Between a man and a rat.
>
> JAKOB: There's no
> Faith in Gettner, that's evident: I see
> No doubt of which of the two is worthy.
> I can't believe in a spiritual democracy.
>
> (3:99)

The act ends with Jakob's warning, "No good will come of Gettner," to which the countess replies, "That may be so" (3:101), but essentially she does believe in a spiritual democracy. Belmann in act 2 repeats his earlier speech on how the countess "undemandingly" causes lives to "make and unmake themselves" but adds, "One man the Countess will never change / By her divine interference: / Ten kroner against Gettner's chances" (3:125). Yet the countess continues to offer chances of change to Gettner to the end. After Stefan's shooting, she asks him for his arm in token of forgiveness and protection, but he does not respond; Belmann's wager remains in doubt to the last moment.

This divine aspect of the countess's role is clear and is marked by Janik's reference, "Peace may go in search of the one soul / But we are not at peace" (3:92). Fry confirmed that the New Testament parables found in Luke 15 underlie the plot of *Dark*.[3] The closest analogy is with the well-known para-

ble of the good shepherd, who leaves his flock to go in search of the one sheep
that was lost. The other two parables—about the rejoicing over the return of
the prodigal son and about the lady who turned her whole house upside
down in seeking one lost coin—are also relevant, especially in the resentment
felt by the prodigal's brother, which parallels the hostility felt by the "respect-
able" characters for Gettner. In purely spiritual terms, the saved souls have
achieved godliness and cannot be diminished in any way by the search for the
lost soul. In the material analogies, however, the rest of the flock seem to the
reader to be in danger, and the prodigal's brother feels neglected. Just so do
the countess's guests feel threatened by Gettner's incriminating presence—
with some reason in material terms. The countess, however, is concerned only
with the spiritual level, the "true world":

> I give you one promise: I shall never make
> Myself, or my friends, my way of life
> Or private contentment, or any
> Preference of my nature, an obstacle
> To the needs of a more true and living world
> Than so far I have understood.
>
> (3:93)

In short, she will do what she sees as right if it kills her—and if it kills her
friends.

This intransigence necessarily affects the presentation of the countess's
character. Apart from her divine significance, she is herself a human being
moving toward death. Her security in goodness noted by Gettner—she
"managed to find a stability / Beside which any despair was condemned to
hesitate" (3:108)—has perhaps deluded even her into confusing the material
with the spiritual. In a long speech, she explains a development taking place
in her as her illness removes her into "some remote evening, some no-man's
country" (3:86), symbolized by the colonel's commandeering of her house:

> You teach me to let the world go, Colonel.
> I've known this house so long,
> Loved it so well
> The hours as they came and went, were my own people . . .
> The years occupied themselves about me.
> The house was perpetual; it was the stars
> Which turned and fled. You see how well you have done

> To remind me my only privilege
> Was to go about a vanishing garden.
>
> (3:116)

But as far as her own life is concerned, the detachment bred by her illness is premature; she has to concern herself again with the life and death of others. It is important that her personal suffering at Gelda's temptation by Gettner and Stefan's shooting should be given due weight, and here much is left to the actress and little offered by the text or stage directions. During Gettner's drunken tormenting of Count Peter, she makes only a two-line attempt at restraint and otherwise remains silent, but Fry intended her distress and fear to be evident. When Stefan is shot, she exercises great self-control, but this and her concern to protect Gettner from the guards should not conceal her anguish; and in fact the inner conflict is dramatized in her collapse, evidently retrieved only by willpower: "I can stand, I can welcome him. I need no help" (3:139).

In some ways the countess has the irritatingly singleminded goodness of a St. Joan, though she disclaims the maid's naiveté: "I know the true world and you know I do" (3:82). When that goodness takes the form of seeming to care only for the spiritual potential of humanity and not caring about their physical well-being, the countess's character becomes even more irritating. Theoretically we may accept the superiority of spiritual over material values, but onstage, as in life, concern for the immediate safety of one's friends is a more sympathetic quality. Belmann is restrained in pointing out that the rescue of Gettner has endangered her guests—"May we presume to doubt your wisdom and care for us?" (3:84)—a conflict soon given a narrower focus in the choice she is asked to make between Gettner and Count Peter.

It is important, then, that some conflict should be evidently taking place within the countess herself and that she should show both a convincing dedication to a truer world and due suffering at the real fear and possible harm she is inflicting on her household. It was questioned whether Edith Evans achieved this as well as she undoubtedly managed the magnetic charm of the countess, and the problem may lie at least partly in the weighting of the text toward charm and away from the inner conflict Fry also intended to be there. Certainly there is plenty of charm written into the countess's part and its context. The opening of the play builds up her character before she appears, as does the centering of attention and dialogue upon her when she first enters. Her apparent frivolity, which partly depends on her indifference to the material preoccupations of her friends, amuses them as it amuses the audience, as when she dismisses in a trivial concession the factor that made her wandering into a blizzard so dangerous: "It was all a very simple matter, / Only complicated by the weather" (3:83). At her specious persuasion that Gettner's desertion has changed into benefit, Colonel Janik confirms the frivolous image: "That, madam, is woman's logic" (3:117). And the evident skill with which she tries to get her own way by indirections—such as the singing of the soldiers' song "Thomasina"—rather than by serious lectures adds to the lighthearted effect.

At least twice her friends mistakenly think that some personal emotional motives underlie her determined activities. One occurs when Gettner assumes that only secret love for himself could have inspired her, and the audience is able to laugh at his ludicrously hurt pride on hearing that she hardly even likes him. Another occurs when she registers alarm and horror in hearing that Gettner has escaped on her horse, Xenophon, but Jakob's attempts to console her apparent concern for Gettner are again amusingly undercut as he finds her concern is for the horse: "I wish he hadn't taken Xenophon. / Xenophon's got a saddle gall" (3:152). Evidently it would be easy to make the mischievous, confident aspect of the countess the whole of the character, especially as her reaction to stressful situations is either silence, or rational or irrational persuasion, not lamentation or recrimination.

The other main character, Gettner, is more clearly revealed by the text. Although at one level he stands for Everyman, his individual personality is strong and far removed from the average. Belmann calls him "that invertebrate, that self-drunk, drunken, shiftless, heartless, / Lying malingerer" (3:70), and from a defiant, assertive pose on his arrival, he moves to a shameless self-preservation in the face of danger:

> . . . I'll not die to oblige anybody;
> Nor for the sake of keeping up
> Decent appearances. Before I do
> I'll get down on all fours, foot-kissing,
> Dust-licking, belly-crawling,
> And any worm can have me for an equal,
> Rather than I should have no life at all.
>   (3:86)

However much Belmann and Stefan insult him, he goes into hiding with an undignified plea to them: "Lie, lie! O Christ, lie for me!" (3:90). Although he claims that honesty is his one virtue, his blunt admissions of his faults seem aimed as much to outrage his opponents as to a love of truth. Egotism is the

trait that unifies both cowardice and reckless gestures, a trait underlined in a
radio production by repeated emphasis on the recurrent *me* of his speeches.
Egotistic jealousy is one of his less attractive qualities; it promotes his renewed
relationship with Gelda in that we see him start accusing Count Peter as soon
as he sees her: "Is he a fool, / Your good husband?" (3:77). Similarly his reaction to the news that his former pursuer, Janik, is in turn being hidden by
the countess is the jealous, "What claim has Janik on this house? / What do
you owe to Janik?" (3:159). But he is only wormlike enough to make the
point that even he can be regarded as worthy of hope. He also has the non-
wormlike aspects that prevent him from ever being content with his lowli-
ness. In his case, a sense of something beyond the material world has come to
him through his writing. He was briefly a writer of great talent and aspired to
create literature like the numinous universe he perceived around him:

> Reality itself, with wonder and power
> Calls for the sound of great spirits
> And mocks us with a wretched human capacity.
> Each day has shone full on me. I have senses,
> Nerves, and mind. Out of this conjunction
> One would suppose there might be born
> Words nearly like the world. Yet no;
> I wrote frustration syllable by syllable.
>
> (3:109)

The universe represents a silent expectation of what Gettner considers to be
impossible, the expansion of mere inadequate humanity to equal the majesty
of creation:

> . . . we're made in no fit proportion
> To the universal occasion . . .
> And very ludicrous it is to see us,
> With no more than enough spirit to pray with,
> If as much, swarming under gigantic
> Stars and spaces.
>
> (3:108)

His talent seems to him a mockery because it has fallen short of the perfection
he sought:

> . . . I preferred
> To stay silent, since it wasn't for me

> To recreate one word fit to stand
> Beside reality, unhumiliated.
>
> (3:110)

Gettner's resentment is a sign of his inability to be merely a worm; his lost-
ness lies in his deliberate turning away from these divine challenges, from
expectations.

Most of the other characters have a commitment to some kind of ideal beyond "undisturbed breathing." The three friends, Kassel, Belmann, and
Jakob, visit the countess on Thursdays for the express purpose of discussing
the moral and ethical aspects of philosophy. Kassel represents the voice of
moderation and common sense, but Belmann and Jakob are more extravagant. Jakob is young and impulsive, and his idealism leads him to idolize the
countess and romantically challenge Belmann to a duel for implying criticism
of her, a challenge not taken at all seriously by the other two. He cries, "At
least I can show myself / What these evenings have meant to me . . . I'm
only / Concerned with this moment of loyalty" (3:72). Ridiculous though
the gesture is, it shows his anxiety to aspire to something outside and beyond
himself.

Belmann is an older and more confident man, given to ironic comment.
Fry thought of him as a Viennese intellectual, possibly an art critic, and he
turns a deliberate, logical attention upon other people and their behavior:

> A man can't know
> How to conduct himself towards another man
> Without the answer to certain basic questions.
> What does the man choose to believe? What good
> And evil has he invented for himself?
> In short, how has he made himself exist?
> And then, the crux of it all,
> Does his chosen existence agree
> With the good and evil I invent for myself?
>
> (3:78)

Kassel tells him, "You're being pompous, Belmann," but he is stating his
view that existence depends on a system of values. Earlier he has said, "A man
has to provide his own providence / Or there's no knowing what religion
will get hold of him" (3:70). This emphasis on "self" and "own" is not a sign
of egotism but of resistance to any merely circumstantial pressures upon his
sense of right and wrong. Evidently, however, Belmann's values differ from

the countess's in that as a humanist and atheist, he relies on himself to discover what is right rather than consciously looking to divine guidance. Colonel Janik, too, is obviously fired by an idealism beyond himself, though his aspirations are for a social and political improvement for Hungary rather than for a spiritual advance for humanity. By the countess's standards, he and Jakob are directing their idealism wrongly in that they are perpetuating violence rather than creating improvement.

The countess's "perfect and upright family" (3:106) adheres to truth and honor. Her son-in-law, Count Peter, is as ready as she is to come to the help of others and pursues the unspectacular course he believes in without indulging in the heroics of Jakob or Gettner in his rebel period:

> I remain, if you like, the fool
> Of my own faith and fallibility,
> And Hungary scorns me; there's no comparison . . .
> . . . For me there's nothing to show;
> But indeed there can be love without evidence.
>
> (3:97)

He is even able to wait and reserve judgment on Gettner's relationship with Gelda, having faith that it can cause no real harm to him, "nothing essential." Fry said that "Peter has the virtues admirable for immediate practical purposes and shows signs of increasing in them."[4] When he is temporarily inspired to fight for the Hungarians during their brief encounter with the Austrians, he decides on reflection that he still rejects violent rebellion as a means to an end, although he has gained insight into the feelings of the Hungarians. Stefan, young and impulsive and partly motivated in his dislike of Gettner by his love and admiration of his mother and Count Peter who are suffering because of the deserter, also tries violent means to free his family from the imposition, and this, Gelda says, forces her into reestablishing her former values.

Gelda herself is a rather shadowy character. Her detour into Gettner's influence is short and, though understandable if Gettner is seen to have a visible magnetism for her, strikes the audience as somewhat blinkered when her husband is in the background in captivity and danger and latterly wounded. Here Fry felt he had been trying to imply too many things at once in the character. In spite of the annulment, he meant Gelda as a Roman Catholic to see her first marriage as still in a way existing, though this is not spelled out. Her lack of natural concern for Peter, such as Hilda feels for Roderic in *Venus*, is puzzling although necessary for the episode to function as a challenge to the countess. Otherwise, like Rosabel in *Venus*, Gelda is present onstage but silent, a difficult task of interpretation for the actress.

The Dark Is Light Enough is subtitled "A Winter Comedy," the third of Fry's seasonal comedies. Its setting is winter, and the death of the year is mirrored in the death of the central character. Death is presented here more soberly than in the spring and autumn plays, where it is merely a cause of terror. Tegeus-Chromis in *Phoenix* had said that "death is a kind of love" (2:14), and the countess expounds the theme more fully. Death, she says, gives value to life; without death, nothing would be more worth mentioning than anything else:

> Protect me
> From a body without death. Such indignity
> Would be outcast, like a rock in the sea.
> But with death, it can hold
> More than time gives it, or the earth shows it.
> I can bear to think of this:
> I can bear to be this, Jakob,
> So long as it bears me.
>
> (3:153)

Paradoxically, a deathless life would reduce humanity to less than animal level, to a mere endless, undifferentiated, unimportant existence, like a rock. The countess's death is prepared even before we know of her illness by her detachment, though this is temporarily interrupted by the revolutionary excitement of the plot; and it is brought nearer by her exile from her house, where custom has created an illusion of permanence. Here, as she thanks Colonel Janik for waking her from this illusion, her description of the deceptive cycle of time significantly omits winter, which brings death:

> Summer would end, surely, but the year fell
> For my sake, dying the golden death
> As though it were the game to put
> Hands over my eyes and part them suddenly
> When primroses and violets lay
> Like raindrops on a leaf
> In the beginning of Spring.
>
> (3:116)

The "golden death" of autumn is not the true death of winter, but it is to winter that she now has come. In the cycle of the Christian year, winter brings
Christmas and the birth of Christ. Although no explicit claim is made that
the death of the countess will bring her rebirth in another life, she promises
not to leave Gettner until she can love him, and in offering this support she
adds, "I don't mean / Necessarily here" (3:165), indicating that she expects
to continue to watch over him from the state beyond death.

Several critics noticed that the language of *Dark* was "wintry" compared
with the exuberance of the spring and autumn comedies. In the *Observer,* Ivor
Brown remarked that the dramatist "has been very much more sparing of his
flowers of speech."[5] Harold Hobson also saw a change: "Now the verse is
vaguer, less like an illuminated missal, less astounding, more subservient to
the matter in hand."[6] And the *Punch* critic similarly said, "The verse is lovely
but bent more closely to the rise and fall of the story."[7] It is difficult to be sure
what they meant by closeness or subservience to the subject matter, but
clearly all have noticed the diminution in the amount of imagery. Even the
countess is quite sparing with metaphor, though she makes use of all kinds of
imagery at times. Her extended simile describing Gettner's uncomfortably
transitional position is as consciously elaborate as any of Mendip's:

> Richard sometimes reminds me of an unhappy
> Gentleman, who comes to the shore
> Of a January sea, heroically
> Strips to swim, and then seems powerless
> To advance or retire, either to take the shock
> Of the water or to immerse himself again
> In his warm clothes, and so stands cursing
> The sea, the air, the season, anything
> Except himself, as blue as a plucked goose.
>   (3:120)

More briefly she illustrates the difference between fact and truth by a new
version of an old analogy:

> Fact? Bones, Colonel. The skeleton
> I've seen dangling in the School of Anatomy
> Is made of facts. But any one of the students
> Makes the skeleton look like a perfect stranger.
>   (3:117)

Symbolism and imagery to do with music, as in the other plays, are important in suggesting the potential harmony of human beings with the eternal. The soldiers' mouth organ and dancing enable the exiled household to recover from Gettner's provocative behavior and avert a threatened conflict— "Music would unground us best" (3:131)—and the countess makes contact with the human reality of the soldiers by learning their song, "Thomasina"; later the song is used to distract Janik from his self-destructive despair.

Most of the longer speeches, however, rely on balance and rhythm rather than on imagery for their effect. One example of the adaptation of syntax to subject matter occurs when the countess first opposes Colonel Janik, beginning with three short, clear sentences challenging his military decisiveness: "I have no weapons to prevent you, Colonel. / The house will go down before you like matchwood. / Your victory will be complete, if not glorious" (3:93). But the structure changes to a long, complex, winding sentence as she embarks on her own indirect, clever persuasion of the colonel:

> Though I wonder you should think
> So unhopefully of your own argument
> That you meekly and unmanfully give in
> To violence, when . . .
>   (3:93)

Similarly Gettner has a set-piece speech claiming that he joined the Hungarian nationalist army in resistance to the Sunday church bells:

> Bash, crash, take that for your damned impudent
> Soul, they said: in the name of the Father, the Son,
> And the Holy Ghost, bash, bash: we'll lay you
> Flat in the mud of Crown Prince Rudolph Street,
> You dust.
>   (3:78–79)

Here the language is following not the sense so much as the sound, the irregular pauses and runs, jerks and hesitations of hand-rung bells, as well as the aggressive energy of clapper striking metal.

Within the terms of seasonal comedy that Fry set up for himself, the element of wintry imagery is not as insistent or striking as, for instance, that of autumn in *Venus*. The most chilling reference to winter is perhaps the half-joking comparison of Gettner to the swimmer by a January sea, which he picks up again, in "To take the cold sea in a courageous plunge" (3:129), but otherwise the benevolent aspect of winter prevails, with snow mercifully covering blots on the landscape:

> . . . a redeemed land, uncrossed by any soul
> Or sound, and always the falling perfection
> Covering where we came, so that the land
> Lay perfect behind us, as though we were perpetually
> Forgiven the journey.
>
> (3:80)

Winter unites with death in redeeming instead of threatening human life.

In spite of its wintriness, then, there can be no doubt that the play is a comedy rather than a drama of suspense. The comic tone is established by the humorous bickering of the chorus of guests who are onstage most of the time. Belmann particularly exploits shades of meaning in his feud with Jakob:

> BELMANN: . . . don't question my integrity.
>
> JAKOB: Very well; I call you a liar.
>
> BELMANN: Well, so I sometimes am.
> But don't question my integrity.
>
> (3:72)

Or he deliberately diminishes Gettner by his choice of words: "We thought / You played games in a different alley now" (3:76). Bella, the countess's servant, has a fine line in deflating commentary; she parries the guests' reproaches with, "If I could always do what's impossible I should have very great advantages" (3:72), and when told to forget about Gettner, retorts, "What's he ever done good enough to forget?" (3:141). And although Janik, Count Peter, Gelda, and Stefan are serious characters with little comedy in their dialogue, the two major characters display a constant wit. Gettner's mischievous desire to shock the guests makes him a comic instead of, or as well as, a contemptible character, and we have seen how the countess's inconsequentiality makes her humorously exasperating to her friends.

The play ends with a death, and perhaps with the prospect of another, for Gettner's chances of escaping alive from the vindictive Austrians must be slim, but it retains its claims to be a comedy because of the texture of the dialogue and the final sense of reconciliation. The play title comes from a quotation from J. H. Fabre on the migration of butterflies, which fly through dark and storm; butterflies, like single-minded and trusting human beings, achieve "the end of their pilgrimage" in spite of the darkness and storm of ad-

versity: "The darkness is light enough . . ." (3:64). The countess is prepared
for and resigned to her death, without having suffered tragically to reach this
state of readiness, and Gettner's last-minute heroism is a triumph over the
wretched, if amusing, selfishness of the rest of the play. In the radio version,
Fry wrote more lines to reinforce the importance of Gettner's redemption,
unworthy though he is. "If there's any measuring to be done," the countess
tells Gettner, who is bitterly recognizing the smallness of her estimate of him,
"It's in the honesty of the struggle / Between the dark and the light. / We
don't need to despair." The countess has persuaded him, and perhaps temporarily the audience, to see events in the context of a truer life, and on those
terms, these deaths contribute to a happy ending.

Chapter Eight

This Is No Winter Now:
A *Sleep of Prisoners*

A Sleep of Prisoners was produced only three years after the long-hatched *Firstborn* and shorter *Thor*, the previous religious plays, but it is quite different from either and different again from the seasonal comedies. It was commissioned by the Religious Drama Society at the instance of E. Martin Browne for the Festival of Britain celebration of 1951. This was taking place exactly one hundred years after the Victorian Great Exhibition, which had asserted Britain's preeminent claims to industrial, technological, and scientific advancement. The 1951 festival was making a similarly positive claim about Britain's recovery from World War II and the years of austerity that had followed. The main festival, centered on Battersea Park, stressed the newest and most startling scientific discoveries and futuristic design. Fry's play, with its framework of soldiers at war and its dream sequence of biblical episodes, was not in step with the purposeful, forward-looking ideology of the festival (although there was no obligation on participants to conform to any central philosophy).

A Sleep of Prisoners is in many ways retrospective. It looks back to the war and warns about the persistence of violent attitudes in humanity, both in and out of military situations. There was no solution to the problem of war unless these attitudes could be changed. In his dedicatory letter to Robert Gittings, recollecting the situation in the thirties, Fry said, "We were talking even then, as we are talking, with greater instancy, now, of the likelihood of war. And I think we realized then, as we certainly now believe, that progress is the growth of vision: the increased perception of what makes for life and what makes for death" (3:3). The play, then, is offering a small dissenting voice to the material optimism of the Festival of Britain in suggesting that true progress lies in the improvement of values, not in technology.

As *Sleep* begins, four soldiers (three privates and a corporal) are imprisoned in a church. Fry said he took the hint for this situation from the history of a church at Burford near where he was living, where a mutinying Leveller contingent of the Parliamentary army were imprisoned in 1649, three ringleaders later being shot. The contemporary language of the play and the references to airplanes, cigarettes, and bomb holes fix the period in the twentieth century, but otherwise, the enemy is referred to only by the nickname Fry has coined, "towzers," so the war could be any war at any time or place. Within this framework, in a series of four dreams the soldiers reenact four stories from the Old Testament: Cain's murder of Abel, David's conflict with Absalom, Abraham's near sacrifice of Isaac, and the ordeal of Shadrac, Meshac, and Abednego in the fiery furnace.

The fluid, episodic structure of the play, which in outline sounds simple, is in fact a complicated design in that the four dreams have different relations to the dreamers: "each of four men is seen through the sleeping thoughts of the others, and each, in his own dream, speaks as at heart he is, not as he believes himself to be" (3:3). In other words, each of the four soldiers dreams one dream in which he reveals his real self and also his biased view of those of his comrades who have a role in his dream. It is not necessarily clear to the reader whose dream is which because this is only hinted in the preliminary dream words of the dreamer. The first dream, for example, is dreamed by the oldest private, Meadows, who has the role of God, but he has little to say during the dream, which is dominated by Cain and Abel, and the reader (and perhaps the audience) might well feel that little is revealed of Meadows at heart. One critic mentions that the first production used "a rather elaborate series of spotlights,"[1] and Fry stresses that a strong spotlight on the dreamer with differential lighting for the dreamed characters is essential for conveying this point of view in performance.

The common theme uniting the episodes is much clearer. The demonstration of the violence people inflict on each other runs through the dreams, different motives in turn being singled out for dramatization. The ground for the dreams is prepared in the waking introductory section during which the tired soldiers settle into their church-prison, and hot-tempered Dave King all but strangles the irritatingly frivolous Peter Able. Some of Dave's destructiveness is instinctive, a volcano in his personality, some judicial, in that he tries to justify his readiness to fight: "The world's got to have us. Things go wrong. / We've got to finish the dirty towzers" (3:13). In the dreams, however, the "enemy" is often brother or son, and the play works its way toward the argument that the unity of humanity must outweigh its divisions. Corporal Joseph Adams, an unimaginative, commonsensical, efficient follower of orders, is opposed to individual violence but promotes institutionalized warfare. Meadows, the oldest of the four, who has concealed his age in order to join the army, takes little part in the conflicts, but as an onlooker he has a commentary that suggests a different level of understanding, a function ex-

panded toward the end when he offers explicit positive guidance to the transfigured men in the furnace, suggesting that humanity must break out of the
cycle of conflict and domination.

The introductory section—this and the first three dreams are roughly the
same length—sets the pattern for the dramatic development of the following
episodes. Weariness and tension balance as the soldiers make up their straw-
filled palliasses, and then the tension flares into crisis as Dave attacks Peter.
The violence is followed by a relaxation, with mixed feelings of guilt, self-
justification, and contrition on Dave's part, and relief for the others, feelings
that dominate in turn in the dreams according to the result of the violence.
Violence, not disobedience, is the most destructive and self-destructive sin.
Although the first dream begins with Meadows as God in dialogue with
Adam, played by Corporal Joe Adams, Adam seems more a bewildered vic-
tim than the disobedient cause of the fall of mankind. The murder of Abel by
Cain eclipses Adam's fault.

Meadows introduces his dream by his words spoken in sleep: "No, no, no.
I didn't ask to be God" (3:16). The essential self revealed here is not that he
sees himself as God or has delusions of grandeur of any kind but, Fry intended, rather that he is essentially responsible, even burdened with a sense of
responsibility. Meadows remains on his bunk while his dream figures move
before him. The dream reenacts Dave's outburst closely, except that the result is fatal, in the similarly instinctive, unpremeditated anger of Cain at
Abel's provocation. In the introduction, Peter had deliberately continued
playing the organ in the loft in spite of Dave's increasingly exasperated protests, rising to, "Come down . . . What for? . . . Because I said so!" (3:7). In
the dream, Peter-Abel is similarly teasing Cain from the "hills," again provoking the exchange, "Come down . . . What for? . . . Because I said so!"
(3:18). In spite of Adam's protest, the murder takes place, and Cain has his
own horror and guilt confirmed and symbolized by the curse of Cain, a punishment that represents the more tormenting remorse in his own soul. In his
dream, Meadows sees the irritating irresponsibility that causes Peter's downfall and Dave's potential repentance.

In the second dream, Dave, the dreamer, is King David, struggling to force
his frivolous son, Absalom, to take sides, to agree that evil exists and that evil
men are enemies. Peter-Absalom refuses to accept this, claiming that anything can be excused or overlooked for the sake of amusement and good company: "What is / A little evil here and there between friends?" (3:28). This is
how Dave sees Peter in the waking world—as someone who ignores the harsh
necessities of wartime. King David's argument is painful necessity—the need
to eliminate those who will not take sides, who betray. At heart Dave is not an

instinctive killer but is convinced of the justice of his actions. Corporal Adams as Joab encourages this clear-cut classification of behavior; the king's withdrawal of protection from Absalom—"He has to be counted with them" (3:31)—is a condemnation to death. The dream world of David and Absalom is half-biblical, half-modern. Absalom offers a cigarette and is cut down with a tommy gun as he hangs from the ledge of the pulpit. Afterward comes the relapse into regret and remorse for the king. What has been gained? "Are we ever sure it's the victory?" (3:32). Joab takes refuge in the orders of others without thinking for himself. He evades the issue: "I can't be held responsible for everything" (3:32). The murderous climax of the dream is never satisfactory; it never solves the problems.

Peter's dream presents himself as the boy, Isaac, whom God has told his father, Abraham, to sacrifice. Peter feels like a boy in the world but like Meadows understands the motives of his less introspective comrades. Dave, as Abraham, is seen by Peter as even less willing to allow the destruction of his son than he was as King David, the command being a test of his obedience. More significant to the theme of the play is the usual typological interpretation of this story as a prefiguring of the crucifixion, with two separate messages: the great sacrifice God makes of his own son to save humanity and the redemption effected by the substitution of the crucified Christ instead of the eternal death of the rest of humanity, as here the ram is substituted for Isaac. The death of Christ is the only necessary sacrifice; further killing of enemies, heretics, and criminals is not necessary. Adams is the angel, the rescuer, as he had been when Dave was strangling Peter, the messenger of God, still fulfilling orders, but this time his "new instructions" give life to Isaac, countermanding the sacrifice and requiring instead the death of the ram.

After the reprieve of Isaac, Meadows appears in the guise of a (nonbiblical) donkey-man with a donkey called Edwina, suggesting a different perspective on the human life Isaac has so nearly lost. Again, as in the waking struggle, he is a rescuer. He gives Peter a ride back to his bunk, bringing associations of boyishness and donkey rides on the beach, but the primary significance is of the donkey as flesh being ridden by the spirit, a temporary mount that the spirit discards after death but still needs in this world. Fry had in mind the words of St. Francis at his death when he referred to his own body as "brother ass."[2]

Corporal Adams has the last dream, the longest and one that moves away from the common pattern of the others. Here the soldiers are not divided into winners and losers, executioner and victim. Adams is at first alone on the sea, where he shows his true self, essentially anxious and insecure, behind the protective armor of military orders. In the production, he remains on his bunk until the dream becomes the common dream of all the men. From his position he cheers on an exhausted Peter and Dave on a march through the pouring rain into a captivity that perhaps echoes the start of their present imprisonment. To him, the others are weaker, younger men who need his practical and physical help.

The dream then becomes a nightmare mixture of imprisonment and the day of judgment. They are inspected by Nebuchadnezzar, their unseen captor, "him with one eye," by which Fry meant to indicate the Blakean "single vision" of purely material power. Suddenly they find themselves in the flames of the furnace. They are bound and helpless but find, like Shadrac, Meshac, and Abednego, whose names they have been given, that they are not affected by the terrifying fire. At this point Meadows appears; he seems to know more about their predicament, just as he has been outside and awake during much of the dreaming. As one of them, he explains, "I can't get out alone." Individual struggle is not the answer. "The flames are men: all human," says Peter. "Breath and blood chokes and burns us. This / Surely is unquenchable? It can only transform. / There's no way out. We can only stay and alter" (3:54). Meadows urges sufferance instead of violent action and, to help human endurance in adversity, a discovery of the purposes of God: "The enterprise / Is exploration into God" (3:55). As the positive message takes shape, urging attention to nonmaterialistic, nonviolent methods of dealing with wrong, Meadows emerges from the dream state, and his speech moves to naturalistic expostulation:

> Where are you making for? It takes
> So many thousand years to wake,
> But will you wake for pity's sake?
> Pete's sake, Dave or one of you,
> Wake up will you? Go and lie down.
> Where do you think you're going?
>   (3:55)

One by one the soldiers emerge from the dream and return to their bunks. With their ritual but optimistic goodnights—"God bless . . . Rest you merry . . . Hope so. Hope so . . ." (3:57)—and the sound of church clock and distant bugle, the play ends.

The structure and the meaning of *Sleep* are closely united. Useless human violence becomes more defensive, more reluctant with each of the three first dreams, and is rejected as irrelevant in the last dream, where the apparently engulfing violence of the furnace is recognized not as the single act of an enemy but as the human condition. Fry, however, was more concerned with showing the dream views of his characters, and therefore within this framework, the biblical figures are phantoms rather than individuals learning from experience. Yet the effect on the audience is to convey the increasing reluctance to solve problems by force. In the last dream, however, Meadows is not a phantom but is speaking for Fry when he outlines the philosophy of goodness that negatively "forbears," that is, endures without violent reaction, against wrong, and positively "grows and makes, and bravely / Persuades, beyond all tilt of wrong" (3:54). "Goodness" is a shorthand for "the longest stride of soul men ever took" (3:55) in which humanity develops to a new pattern of life more consonant with God's hidden image of human fulfillment. This is a "deed of time," an evolutionary step, moving from the summit of physical evolution to a spiritual evolution, which Meadows calls "exploration into God" (3:55).

The theme of violence is united with the theme of human evolution, as in *Thor* and *Venus*. In the Cain and Abel dream, Peter already guesses the possibility of some further meaning to life beyond the material:

> Here we are, we lean on our lives
> Expecting purpose to keep her date,
> Get cold waiting, watch the overworlds
> Come and go, question the need to stay
> But do, in an obstinate anticipation of love.
>   (3:19)

By "purpose" he says he means "the justification." Dave-Cain, on the other hand, is arrested at the lower level—"Amply the animal is Cain, thank God" (3:19)—and he rejects Abel's unfulfilled state of "waiting" as unfair:

> So any lion can BE, and any ass,
> And any cockatoo: and all the unbiddable
> Roaming voices up and down
> Can live their lives and welcome
> While I go pestered and wondering down hill
> Like a half-wit angel strapped to the back of a mule.
>   (3:22)

Like the duke of Altair, he is describing the contrast between the established pattern of the animal kingdom and the not-yet-defined state of humanity,

and the mule image looks forward to the reminder of this body-spirit partnership in the donkey-man episode.

The more sophisticated King David tries to fix a logical military order on
society, as Pharaoh Seti did in *The Firstborn*. Although his reasons are inadequate and artificial, Peter-Absalom's objections this time are equally so. He
avoids the problem by denying it:

> But you and I
> Know that we can turn away
> And everything will turn
> Into itself again. What is
> A little evil here and there between friends?
>   (3:28)

This is escapism, not tolerance. "I manage to get out" (3:30), he repeats. If
violence is not the answer, neither is condonement of evil.

As Abraham, Dave sees his role as directed by history: "I am history's wish
and must come true" (3:37). History here means circumstances, the pressure
of events, even the slow movement of spiritual evolution that at a primitive
stage allows hate but will eventually discard the need for hate altogether.

The problem of when to refrain and when to act rightly instead of acting
without thought is the real problem for the average person, as represented by
Dave and Adams:

> And every standing day
> The claims are deeper, inactivity harder.
> But where, in what maze of right and wrong,
> Are we to do what action?
>   (3:54)

As the helpless prisoners in the fiery furnace fall on their knees, Peter cries,
"We shall know!" and Adams adds, "I live. I know I kneel" (3:50). The ultimate test of being is to know one's reliance on God, symbolized by kneeling.
Here Adams is again Adam, the original man or Everyman, achieving his redemption. He lives; the cords of lower, Cain-like animal life "are burnt, drop
off / Like snakes of soot" (3:51). The clearest statement of positive values
comes from Meadows, the "son of man," who in summary explains the po-
tency of good, which eschews both the aggression and retaliation seen in the
earlier dreams and promotes inward change and persistent campaigning
against wrong.

How much of this does the audience grasp after one viewing? Writing in the *Sunday Times*, Harold Hobson perceived that "one realises with a shock which momentarily unseats the values by which one has judged man's strife down the ages, that every time man's blood is shed, for Mr Fry, Our Lord is slain again." But he went on to say, "The play cannot be understood, despite the miracles of clarification that Mr Michael MacOwan has wrought as producer, unless one is willing to give it an attention as close as is necessary to fill up a pool coupon. This reduces its potential audience at a blow by about ninety nine per cent."[3] Similarly T. C. Worsley in the *New Statesman* wrote, "If I understand it rightly (but one cannot expect to grasp a play of this intensity whole at one sitting) the theme is the uses and abuses of action and violence."[4]

Probably the area of difficulty is concentrated toward the end of the play; the early Cain and Abel and David and Absalom episodes clearly plead against brutal solutions to problems. However, the Abraham and Isaac story is more complex in its double reference to the repugnance of human sacrifice and to the beneficence of Christ's redemptive sacrifice. The last scene, in the furnace, is the most difficult; the characters are striving for resolution through a mental struggle expressed by images and absolutes. The argument is not a simple one; their doubts and questions recur in a somewhat circular manner. Dave agrees "I can see / To be strong beyond all action is the strength / To have" (3:53), but then protests, "Who says there's nothing here to hate?" and "But good's unguarded" (3:54). Similarly Peter realizes, "We can only stay and alter" (3:54), but then fears "this fire . . . goes beyond any stretch of the heart" (3:55). There is not a clear sense of final conviction.

Up to this last scene, the development of the characters has helped to clarify the meaning of the play. Private Dave King begins as an apologist for violence and changes most during the dream transformations. Ironically, the kindest view of him comes in the dream of his victim, Peter. His initial waking tendencies to the bestial passions and crude rationalizations of his violence are reenacted in the first two dreams. The second of these is his dream, and here, as King David, he "speaks as at heart he is, not as he believes himself to be" (Preface). Though destructive, his motives are rooted in valid emotions. "Living is caring" (3:28), he tells Absalom. Like Henry in the later *Curtmantle,* he cannot tolerate shades of dissent: "the indecisions have to be decided" (3:29). The relevance to waking life is close; Dave, still in his dream, uses both mythical and real names in the same speech: "Don't do it to me, don't make the black rage / Shake me, Peter . . . Where's your hand? / Be ordinary human, Absalom" (3:29). Again like Henry half-wanting the death of Becket, David half-orders the death of Absalom—"He's with the

enemy. He betrays us, Joab. / He has to be counted with them" (3:31)—
and then suffers agonies of remorse afterward. The king is capable of
misgivings:

> Are you sure it is the victory, Joab?
> Are we ever sure it's the victory?
> So many times you've come back, Joab,
> With something else. I want to be sure at last.
> I want to know what you mean by victory.
> Is it something else to me?
>
> (3:32)

Neither Dave nor his Cain persona could have made this distinction. By
the time Peter dreams him as Abraham, his allegiance to "necessary hatred" is
softened, and he recognizes its destructiveness clearly:

> I am history's wish and must come true,
> And I shall hate so long as hate
> Is history, though, God, it drives
> My life away like a beaten dog.
>
> (3:37)

Here the killer is the victim of circumstances, not a motive force. Finally, in
the furnace, he relapses to his original thoughtless outbursts—"Let me, dear
God, be active / And seem to do right, whatever damned result" (3:47)—
before he completely reverses it with, "I can see / To be strong beyond all action is the strength / To have" (3:53).

Peter, on the other hand, begins with an attitude of tolerance that shades
into inertia and escapism. As Dave parodies him, "Don't let's mind /
What happens to anybody, don't let's object to anything" (3:10). As Abel,
he expresses the laudable human aspiration for something beyond the material world, but Dave dreams only of his complementary vice of indifference to the society he has to live in. In his own dream as Isaac, he is sensitive
and responsive, instinctively rejoicing in life and shrinking from the incom-
prehensibility of death, like the boy Rameses looking at the dead bird:
"Surely there's no reason for us to be / The prisoners of the dark?" (3:38).
He is voicing the eternal cry of humanity, to be answered by the Christian
redemption prefigured in his own sacrificial role. In the final dream, he
shows both weakness and strength. It is he who wants to drop out of the
dream march and has to be upheld by the others, crying, "I can believe any-

thing except / The monster" (3:47). Refusal to believe in evil is an Absalom-excuse for avoiding action, just as Dave believes in evil as an excuse for destructive action, but Peter realizes in the end that escapism must be rejected: "We can only stay and alter" (3:54).

Adams is a lesser character. His dual role as a corporal, preserving peace and unity among his own men and preparing hostility against the enemy, is reflected in the first dream where, as Adam, he contains all the potential of the human race in his person and sees the internal conflict beginning in his sons: "I made them both, the fury and the suffering, / The fury, the suffering, the two ways / Which here spreadeagle me" (3:23). Adam is an observer, a figure of authority with no real power. "I am a father unequipped to save" (3:24), he says. As Joab, he executes David's commands without interposing his own judgment—"I've done my best. / I can't be held responsible for everything" (3:32)—and as the angel who transmits "new instructions" to Abraham, he similarly mirrors his military role as obedient follower of other people's orders. In his own final dream, which turns eventually into a communal dream, he, the average man, the "old Adam," is joined by the others whom he represents. Here he plays himself, a corporal, a confused ordinary man who relies on routine and orders. He lies on his imaginary raft and reiterates, "presently you drown . . . / Presently you drown"; his essential insecurity is evident (3:44). Once involved in the practicalities of keeping exhausted men from dropping out of the march, he feels purposeful, but later, when the terror of imprisonment in the furnace wears off, he shares Dave's inability to bear inactivity. His last dream words suggest, however, that he has recognized an obligation to discriminate between the orders inposed on him: "Strange how we trust the powers that ruin / And not the powers that bless" (3:54).

Meadows is a special case among the four soldiers. He does not develop during the play because he already has wisdom. He begins the dream sequence as God and ends it as the fourth figure that appears in the furnace, usually interpreted as a manifestation of Christ. He plays little part in the second and third dreams, except to appear in the transitional passage as the donkey-man. Here his message of faith in time and eventual progress— "She's slow, / But it's kind of onwards" (3:40)—reflects his later guidance, when he appears through the flames crowing like a cock, intended by Fry to symbolize hope of a new dawn. His long last speech in the final dream draws together the themes of the play and challenges not only the other soldiers but the audience to react to the present period, the "upstart Spring" and its flood of wrong, with their souls and hearts.

Although the themes of *Sleep* are similar to those of the later *Dark,* its language is as inventive as the earlier *Venus* and in the dreams takes on additional license to distort and decorate the dialogue in keeping with the ambiguous identities and motives of the dream characters. Cain's presentation of himself as a husky, muscular, strapping stripling, passionate and with all his wits about him, is telescoped as "a huscular strapling / With all his passions about him" (3:19)—an example of the Freudian dream economy with language, two or three ideas being expressed at once. Thus, Adams-Angel unites images of bonds and the sea to reflect indissoluble human interdependency when he tells Abraham to undo "these particular" cords "but never all. / There's no loosening, since men with men / Are like the knotted sea" (3:39). The purely descriptive writing is as full of imagery as the earlier plays, Edwina, the donkey, being briefly characterized as "two swimming eyes and a cask of ribs" (3:40), and there are more extended images such as that of the sheets of flame as "a narrow shaking street / Under the eaves of seven-storeyed flames / That lean and rear again" (3:51). Lyrical images express moments of extreme feeling, as when Adam cries, "My heart breaks, quiet as petals falling / One by one" (3:23), and Meadows exclaims, "O God, the fabulous wings unused, / Folded in the heart" (3:53).

The waking passages are simpler though still vivid. Meadows observes that the soldiers are "sleeping like great roots" (3:26), while "there's a howling wind outside plays ducks and drakes / With a flat moon" (3:31). Even within the dreams, the imagery and distortion is varied with weighty simplicity, as in Cain's brief, despairing reply to the biblical accusations that his brother's blood cries out from the ground: "Sir, no: he is silent. / All the crying is mine" (3:24). Different again is the poignant understatement of old Adam, recalling the Fall in the bitterly regretful answers of soldier before Meadows-God as his commanding officer:

MEADOWS:	As you were, Adam.
ADAMS:	No chance of that, sir.
MEADOWS:	As you were, as you were.
ADAMS:	Lost all track of it now, sir . . .
MEADOWS:	I said Let there be love, And there wasn't enough light, you say?
ADAMS:	. . . It was all over and the world was on us Before we had time to take cover.
MEADOWS:	Stand at peace, Adam: do stand at peace.
ADAMS:	There's nothing of that now, sir.

(3:16–17)

The rhythm varies perhaps more noticeably than in Fry's comedies; Abraham's words as he prepares to sacrifice Isaac are ritualistically repetitive:

> I let you go, for the world's own ends
> I let you go, for God's will
> I let you go, for children's children's joy
> I let you go, my grief obeying.
>
> (3:38)

There is Meadows's imitation of the heavy breathing rhythm of his companions—". . . And the breathing; and the breathing; heavy and deep; / Breathing: heavy and deep. / Sighing the life out of you. All the night" (3:26)—and Peter's inexorably slowing, exhausted march—"I wouldn't know. It. Feels. / Damned. Odd. To me" (3:44). By contrast, Absalom's impudent defiance alternates the rhythm of jazzlike long phrases and short, brisk units:

> Beloved, all who pipe your breath
> Under the salted almond moon,
> Hell is in my father's head
> Making straight towards him. Please forget it.
> He sees the scarlet shoots of spring
> And thinks of blood . . .
> Shake hands on it: shake hands, shake hands:
> Have a cigarette and make yourselves at home.
>
> (3:28)

The rhythm of the play varies in pace between frantic dream activity and the intervals of the sleepers' inaction. Harold Hobson found the first production more visually gripping than Fry's earlier plays: "We all know what Mr Fry can do with words. . . . But here Mr Fry flings words, his slaves and his master, aside. He reveals himself capable of charging visual drama with electrical significance." He examines the murder of Abel "before the eyes of Adam, who vainly strives to intervene, but is held back by invisible bonds, and his straining body, with arms outstretched, and head bent forward, suddenly becomes the figure of a man crucified."[5] The church setting and the fluidity of the changing dream landscapes instantly and entirely indicated by mime and language means that the action can proceed without hindrance, as, for example, the pulpit becomes a mountain, then a tree, then an altar of sacrifice. Fry recalled, "I remember feeling a pleasant freedom in writing *A Sleep of Prisoners*" ("Talking of Henry," 188).

Most of the action is dynamic, and the freedom offered by the dream convention seems to have enabled Fry to write only the essence of what he needed, untrammeled by the need for exposition, social conversation, and so forth. In spite of the complaints of contemporary reviewers ("fashionably obscure," said one),[6] the pacifist element in the message now seems clear. There remains, however, the problem of the last scene and its development. Here perhaps the consequences of the philosophy of the play are less clear because they are not enacted (as Gettner enacts the consequences of the countess's philosophy at the end of *Dark*), and whereas *Venus* ended with a satisfactory verbal evocation of the hero's change of attitude, that attitude was capable of being fully conveyed by imagery, whereas the final message of *Sleep* is more complex in what it is saying about sufferance, passive resistance, rejection of self-interest, and exploration into God. In *Sleep* we see the negative forces that must be rejected and then hear a general exhortation to take a "stride of soul," an image less easy to translate than the duke's autumnal optimism. On the other hand, in *Dark*, Fry embodies these positive qualities in the countess, who is then open to charges of improbable perfection, if not priggishness. This is a perennial problem for all writers who want to present negative and positive poles of their beliefs, and after the positive and negative dramatizations in *Dark* and *Sleep*, Fry takes care to make even Saint Thomas Becket a fallible and baffling human being.

Chapter Nine

A Quest for the True Law: *Curtmantle*

Although few of Fry's plays are set in the twentieth century—and two, *Venus* and *Sleep*, have a timelessness that makes each, as Brook said of the former, "not really a contemporary play"—only *Curtmantle* is a truly historical play, dealing with events and characters of the recorded past. The advantage of a historical setting, Fry says, is that "you get a clearer look at what you might call the permanent condition of man" ("Talking of Henry," 189). In the foreword to the play, its two themes are defined as "one a progression towards a portrait of Henry, a search for his reality, moving through versions of 'Where is the King?' to the unresolved close of 'He was dead when they came to him'. The other theme is Law, or rather the interplay of different laws: civil, canon, moral, aesthetic, and the laws of God; and how they belong and do not belong to each other" (3:175). The first of these themes determines the shape of the play with its long time span, but the foreword adds that "though it follows chronology, it is not a chronicle play" (3:174). By this, Fry meant that the play did not try to be inclusive or to break up its material into separate episodes. Instead he aimed at a flow of action, managed by the narrator-participator William, Earl Marshal of England, in whose mind the events are being recalled: "The stage is William Marshal's mind, as though he were remembering the life of Henry" (3:174).

William, the earl marshal, is the only person who is with Henry from beginning to end of the play. Originally he did not appear in the prologue, which stands separate from the main flow of events, but for the English production, he was given an introductory speech "to establish him as the memory in which the action of the play takes place" (3:176). He begins: "Memory is not so harsh as the experience. Who can recall now the full devastation of the time when young Henry Plantagenet first came to his kingdom? Henry Curtmantle, we sometimes called him, with his cloak as short as his need for sleep. His energy was like creation itself; he was giving form to England's chaos, an England that after eight years of civil war had no trade, no law, no conscience" (3:179).

The prologue illustrates this process of transformation. It is separate from the rest of the play because it represents a typical incident, repeated or paralleled probably hundreds of times throughout Henry's lifetime, whereas the events of the play proper are single, usually decisive and unique episodes. Briefly, the prologue shows the confusion and discomfort of the king's lesser servants left to manage as they can in the wake of the king's excursions through a dark, uninhabited, stormy countryside. The more thoughtful among them have a sense of what the king is trying to do. The barber says, "You can tell yourself it's a great benefit to the kingdom. That's the outcome of it. Law and order is the outcome. Haven't you got a memory for the smoke and ruin this land was? Mad, and murderous, and lawless, bleeding away like raw meat" (3:181). But the barber's wife and the huckster are less sure that good will come of their suffering: "He'll march us all to death to get his law and order, though I'll say this, he's sorry for you when you're dead" (3:184). An unfortunate gentleman who blunders into the servants' encampment is seeking justice, and while his complaints show how necessary justice is, his hopes of achieving it are whisked out of reach with the abrupt breaking up of camp because the king has already started out in the dark for a distant town. "Where is the King? Where shall I find the King? A law that's just and merciful! Do I have to walk on for ever, looking for that?" (3:186). Henry gives justice, but his own energy prevents its being as all encompassing as he intends, and this inner contradiction underlies most of Henry's public and private behavior in the play.

For the three acts of *Curtmantle*, William Marshal is mainly an actor in the drama but adds commentary and linking narrative to indicate the passing of time between events, without the formal break of scene divisions. The first long sequence shows the beginning of the rift between Henry and his old friend and chancellor, Thomas Becket. We first see them laughing and joking together; Henry is very much the benevolent and powerful medieval king, and his forceful high spirits are met by Becket's modest but independent friendliness. Queen Eleanor, though out of sympathy with the crude energy of the English court under Henry, can dissolve into laughter at Becket's mimickry of her former husband, pious King Louis of France. This unity is broken by Henry's casual remark to his chancellor: "Which reminds me, Tom: I'm giving you Canterbury. / By your own merit, Archbishop as well as Chancellor" (3:197). The king is so casual because it seems to him a natural, logical move, drawing the dissentient church into the unity he shares with Becket.

Becket disagrees. Church and state are at odds because the state's values are material and the church's are spiritual; this is an essential and inevitable difference reflecting the dual nature of humanity:

> There is a true and living
> Dialectic between the Church and the state
> Which has to be argued for ever in good part.
> It can't be broken off or turned
> Into a clear issue to be lost or won.
> It's the nature of man that argues;
> The deep roots of disputation
> Which dug in the dust, and formed Adam's body.
>
>   (3:199)

The conflict between Henry and Becket, which lasts until Becket's death and perhaps beyond, shows the truth of this analysis.

William Marshal carries the story forward with narrative description of Becket's consecration as archbishop of Canterbury, his narrative interrupted by a short scene with a prostitute, Blae, who is successful in insisting that her little son, Roger, is the king's and should be brought up at the palace. Evidently some time has passed, for we see Henry opening a letter from Becket, who has withdrawn to Canterbury and now writes resigning his chancellorship in order to represent the church single-heartedly. Henry is furious, and we pass straight to a confrontation between the two men. As in the rest of the play, there is no break to mark the passage of time, and unbroken conversations bridge the two incidents. Their confrontation underlines the incompatibility of the priorities of church and state, and the act ends with Henry posed "as though squaring up for a fight" (3:213).

Act 2 is full of conflict for Henry. It traces the development of his quarrel with Becket and shows the cracks appearing in the Plantagenet empire he is seeking to establish. In a strange scene court and church debate the issues of supremacy or independence, surrounded by billowing fog in which the shadows of the participants loom unnaturally above their dwarfed human shapes. Becket begins and ends with a refusal of total obedience to the king, making the reservation "saving our order" (3:279), and the other bishops echo his words. Partway through the argument, however, Henry's rage is so terrifying, along with the threats of the courtiers and the fear of the churchmen, that Becket is persuaded to submit and rely on Henry's goodwill. At this moment of unexpected relief, Henry produces a legal contract of obedience for Becket to sign, a formal document that will tie the hands of the churchmen without room for negotiation—or goodwill. Becket recoils in horror back to his first position, and Henry in revenge unleashes his massive power against him, demanding, for instance, repayment of all the revenues Becket was paid in his chancellor years. This scene of dangerous defiance, which Eleanor rightly compares to a bullfight, is followed by a shorter episode showing Becket's continued obstinacy in spite of a trial convened against him in his absence that has labeled him a traitor.

Nothing is resolved then, but the action now follows a different theme: Eleanor brings the news of the birth of a son to King Louis, signifying a threat and an obstacle to Henry's present and planned power in France. At the same time Eleanor expresses her own resentment of Henry's neglect of her, as both a woman and an experienced politician. This marks one of the troughs of Henry's fortune, and characteristically he at once begins, with a resurgence of energy, to devise a new plan to overcome the problem. In order to strengthen his dynasty, he determines to assign lands to his sons at once and to crown Harry, the eldest, as nominally king alongside himself. As with the attempt to unify church and state, this plan for family unity leads only to worse dissension as the coronation feast of young Harry degenerates into bickering. In spite of Henry's desperate plea for unity, the four boys quarrel jealously, deliberately provoking Henry by praising the now-exiled Becket, and a fight between Harry and Richard is stopped only by the intervention (and wounding) of the illegitimate Roger, Blae's son. At the same time Eleanor announces she is leaving Henry to live on her own lands with Richard. Again the king is discouraged but then forces a new initiative: he will seek a reconciliation with Becket and foil any threat from Louis by a diplomatic alliance. Another smooth transition takes him from the suggestion "Catch him in Normandy" to "And here we stand in Normandy" (3:245) two speeches later. Time has passed, and a reconciliation with Becket has been prepared; Becket himself appears and agrees to return to Canterbury.

This is a turning point in the play, but it is not clear how the crisis comes about. Becket is disappointed that Henry is not returning with him, but no clear motive appears for Becket's next reported actions. In his linking narrative, the marshal suggests that infatuation in the sense of self-destructive foolishness made Becket recommence defiance and confrontation as soon as he reached England. This news provokes another of Henry's blind rages, and the fatal words: "Who will get rid of this turbulent priest for me?" (3:249). The act ends with misery and tension as Henry waits to hear whether the self-appointed executioners have been intercepted. Becket's murder is reported to Henry in semidarkness; his emotions break out as ferociously as his rage as he "steps into the light like a madman" (3:252). Rage is dominant in the complex emotions of this moment as he cries out against the whole world before lapsing into solitary grief.

The switchback variety of Henry's moods and actions throughout the second act arouses an expectation of some change, but act 3 suggests that the Plantagenets, like the Bourbons, learn nothing and forget nothing. After an initial scene of penance and mortification in the dark crypt of Canterbury Cathedral, Henry enters the sunlit Court of Love in Poitou, where Eleanor sits among their three elder sons, and has his soldiers arrest and imprison her. Three years have elapsed between acts 2 and 3, and another fifteen pass during this final act, which is also the shortest, and thus becomes more swiftly paced, the events not flowing with logical connection but seemingly selected from Henry's crowded life. We next see Henry mourning the deaths of young Harry and Geoffrey. Though hostile, they were part of the Plantagenet house whose prosperity was his driving motive; this loss is crushing to his plans. Yet within moments he is rebuffing Richard's overconfident claims to his blessing on his succession. Henry will not accept what is forced on him by others: "I dispose as I choose" (3:262). Like Becket, Eleanor, and others before him, Richard refuses Henry's dominance. The marshal then tells of the years of war as Richard and young Philip of France drive Henry out of his continental possessions one by one, a negation of will that becomes a nightmare. Driven back to his birthplace, Le Mans, Henry gives orders to burn some strategically dangerous hovels and thus causes fire accidentally to catch the town itself; the whole city, the place of his birth and his father's death, burns before his eyes.

This final sequence brings a series of crushing blows to Henry and inexorably reduces him to the lowest state imaginable after his life of pride and domination. He curses God. As in the unintended death of Becket and of Harry and Geoffrey, the world he tries to control has turned and crushed him. Surprisingly, however, he seems about to make yet another energetic recovery, and "suddenly gay as though he were a boy again" (3:266) he plans a clever retreat and regrouping: "Come on; the years are only beginning. We head for Anjou" (3:267). This is not to be permitted. Another betrayal is that of his own body; as he speaks, he is racked with pain and collapses. At this moment Philip of France and Richard take possession of the field unopposed since Henry is not only cornered but physically incapable of movement. Richard taunts his father, but Philip is coolly courteous in demanding Henry's surrender of Richard's lands, a money payment to defray the costs of war, the release of Eleanor, and acknowledgment of Richard as his successor. Compared, for instance, with the fines heaped on Becket, these demands seem fair and even light—but not to Henry's pride. Nonetheless, he has to give way, and when

Richard reveals that Prince John has deserted his father and joined them, his last secret hope of vengeance is destroyed.

Only his bastard son, Roger, and the marshal are with him now, and the latter goes to seek help. As a background to this scene, the common people appear, unseen since the prologue. The townsfolk of Le Mans pass by, refugees from the flames, and Roger finally leaves the delirious king with a few refugees while he fetches a monk to what is evidently Henry's deathbed. The townsfolk are at first awestricken, but when Henry falls back dead, they strip off his clothes and possessions, claiming "this dead fellow owes us a bit of justice" (3:276); the marshal and Roger return, horrified, to find his naked body. This loss of power, physical control, and even decent covering suggests a deliberate punishment for hubris, blasphemy, or some other tragic flaw. Yet there is also a sense of achievement; before his death, Roger comforts him with reminders of the legal system he has devoted his life to building, and afterward an old woman tells them, "He was dead when they came to him" (3:277). The essence of Henry has escaped.

As the extent of this summary suggests, the development of Henry's life story in dramatic form is intensely bound up with events; it is a closely organized sequence of significant actions and decisions. Little of it can be passed over or cut because each episode supports later episodes, contributing to Henry's series of willful acts that end in his lonely defeat. Where in *Lady* or *Venus* different characters had little scenes to themselves where they exemplified both their uniqueness and their illustrations of themes, scenes in *Curtmantle*, as well as showing themes and character, are part of a necessary chain of cause and effect explaining historical consequences.

The essential paradox of Henry is of a man seeking to compose a rigid framework of laws when he himself—his personal life and his rule over his court—proceeds by the arbitrary energy of his will alone. Although the word *justice* is often used, law rather than justice is the main theme because laws can differ and conflict according to their purpose, which is not always justice. The foreword mentions the "interplay of different laws: civil, canon, moral, aesthetic, and the laws of God; and how they belong and do not belong to each other" (3:175). Henry's reign follows a civil war between his mother, only child of Henry I, and her cousin, Stephen of Blois, who seized the throne, a war in which all forms of law had given way to brigandage. Henry's ambition is to establish civil law in a logical system that will approximate to justice in the sense of enforcing accepted rights.

For all his attractive energy and generosity, Henry has a single-mindedness that makes the sword of justice a two-edged weapon. There is little room for tolerance or allowance for mitigating circumstances in his "the day is soon coming when those who deviate will be compelled / Into the common pattern" (3:193). Henry is supremely self-confident about the simplicity of the task, which he sees as recompensing God for any minor offenses:

> We'll make up to Him for it by establishing
> Order, protection, and justice
> For the man who has a shirt or the man who has not.
> A pity the whole of the earth is not to be
> Serene in our keeping.
>
>   (3:201)

All that has to be done is to formulate some unambiguous laws and force people to administer them fairly. He does not see that there may be a difference between opinion and opinion as to what justice, truth, and unity may be. So he imposes his logic on Becket:

> Either there are laws for every man,
> And he is one; or there are no laws for any man.
> The day is vital, and the world can't stand still
> To be cheated, even under cover of God.
>
>   (3:225)

Becket, however, even before he becomes archbishop, already has a sense of the laws of God and sees them conflicting with worldly justice. At the beginning of the first act, he and Henry disagree over the church's exoneration of the criminal canon of Lincoln. Canon law, the codification of certain religious imperatives into legal form, is, as Fry's foreword implies, not the same as God's law; it is more limited, more influenced by the context of the codifiers, and as open to abuse as any other human system. Henry sees canon law as exploited by the ecclesiastical courts to protect the church's servants. Becket goes to the foundation in God's law and like the countess in *Dark* argues that any life must be given every chance, and the maximum time, to make its journey toward spiritual perfection. When Henry later points to the fact that clerics have been spared the penalties that civil courts impose by law on laymen, including "already in my time a hundred murders," Becket replies:

> There would have been two hundred
> If we had hanged the murderers. As it is,
> There are now a hundred men who see we think

Lives of more account than they did: spirits
In trust, which we must never despair of.
(3:217)

To Henry this perpetual forgiveness is an offense against justice and unfair to
"the other honest, poor damned sons of Cain" (3:192). But Becket would extend the fairness in the other direction and perhaps not altogether seriously
retorts, "All right, Henry. / Let's leave the poor damned sons of Cain to God,
then" (3:193). What is a flippant debate during their friendship becomes a
conflict with implications for ultimate power when Becket comes to represent
not just himself but the church. Law may interfere with spiritual development, which must take priority over all else:

This is not under the law, but under grace.
What you see as the freedom of the State
Within the law, I fear, as the enslavement
Of that other state of man, in which, and in
Which only, he can know his perfect freedom.
(3:218)

But Henry takes the view that on earth, obedience in earthly things is due
only to the state, that is, ultimately to him. Equally alien to his concept of
consistant, fixed laws is Eleanor's plea for diversity: "Consider complexity,
delight in difference" (3:226). Ironically Henry and Eleanor accuse the other
of views opposite to those each seems to advocate. Henry condemns Eleanor's
"aesthetic laws" in her court of love as forcing a rigid, destructive pattern on
emotions and relationships, "the unexceptionable dance of what / Has with-
ered within" (3:259); Eleanor warns Henry of the lack of faith and law in his
own chaotic private life:

You who so struggle for order everywhere
Except in your own life.
If anarchy should prove to be a state which is indivisible,
Stretching from your own body across the face of the world,
You have stinging days ahead of you.
(3:231)

The issue of law is contained within the larger theme of unity and diversity: Henry sees the law as unified and unifying while both Becket and
Eleanor are pleading for toleration and variety. In other areas, too, Henry's
dream of unity fades as soon as formulated. Within the family, he insists, in

vain, that "the house is a single thing" (3:232), and "the voice of Plantagenet is one voice" (3:233), but his sons behave according to the prediction: "Each of us against the other" (3:260). The unity of the roles of chancellor and archbishop is a chimera, as Becket points out, because of the different interests involved. The friendship of Henry and Becket is cracked apart in spite of Henry's incredulity: "Tell me how a man who has seen eye to eye with me / Can suddenly look at me as if he was blind?" (3:213). The duality of human nature disrupts the simple pursuit of unity as the marshal remarks, "The simple and reasonable action, at the very moment it came to life, was neither simple nor limited to reason . . . The whole significance of unity was not debated, nor what fires can forge a diverse multitude into one mind" (3:203).

We see the duality causing vexation and dissent, from the French king Louis, "Frayed to ribbons whether to be / A king or an archbishop" (3:196), to the common people who appreciate Henry's laws "as a source of strength" (3:272) but also flock after Becket and kiss the stones he treads on. Henry claims, "The truth is unalterable, the truth being one," but Becket counters, "The truth, like all of us, being of many dimensions" (3:199).

Because he believes in only one truth, one law, one Plantagenet policy, Henry regards Becket's dissent as betrayal—and he feels it as a personal, not political, betrayal. Eleanor is critical of this: "We shall see the kicks and blows of angry men, / Both losing sight of the cause" (3:226), but it is this personal dimension that gives Henry his warmth and attractiveness. Fry was fascinated by Henry's character, and Henry's personal involvement in his policies increasingly adds the tragic dimension to the perennial power struggle of church and state. In act 1, Henry is only twenty-nine, though with long experience of ruling his kingdom, and he sustains his young man's energy almost to the end of the play. Possibly in the first act his optimism is more rash and sweeping as he dismisses Becket's protests merely as a *noli episcopari* gesture. His comment, "You will miss your falcons, of course, if you decide / That blood sports are too secular" (3:199), shows his absolute confidence that any problems with his plans can be no more than superficial. He is still the bold, energetic figure of the prologue who zigzags across England to spring surprise visits of inspection on his judges. The defections of others hurt him; first Becket and then Eleanor turn away, and in spite of his lack of faithfulness to Eleanor, he does not expect her to abandon him: "You were with me all through the time when I was shaping / The nightmare into an empire" (3:239). These blows never lead to self-questioning, but they do bring eventual disillusion:

> At first I could have believed all men
> Were born of an act of love . . .
> . . . Now there aren't
> Many I can look at with much belief
> (3:240)

The audience, however, can see how much Henry is responsible for his own tragedy. After the death of Harry and Geoffrey, he asks, "What did I do to lose them? First their love, / Then their lives?" (3:261) What did he do also to lose Richard and John, Becket and Eleanor? Obviously his attractive qualities have their corresponding vices; his positive energy becomes coercive and domineering. Eleanor early warns Becket, "You and I . . . Have our future state only in a world of Henry" (3:202), and in the third act, young Harry, having temporarily escaped his father, says nervously, "There's only one pulse in Christendom, the one / Self-will, overriding everything: our father!" (3:257). Naturally a powerful, visionary, active medieval king is autocratic and egotistical. Justifiably proud of his achievements, he claims, "There's no anarchy to come worse / Than I've already transformed into good government" (3:190). Foliot asks, "What man dictates the future?" and Henry replies, "In this instance, I do" (3:232–33). Because he believes in only one truth, he makes no attempt to understand the perspective of his victims; for instance, he does not see that his unfaithfulness to Eleanor is insulting or hurtful: "There's nothing to be said. The days are hot; / The thirst on the way demands a little shade, / And fresh water" (3:232). He brutally crushes the boy Harry's resentment of insult: "As it is / You're not fit to lead a crusade of children" (3:244). And he tells Richard, "I dispose as I choose. / By God, you'd better submit to my peace" (3:262).

His power and early success cause him to assume God's favor: "Not a son is born to Louis . . . But four good boys to me. / There's God articulate, if ever a god spoke" (3:190). God's apparent desertion at the end of act 3 is repaid with the same kind of angry retaliation as the human defections:

> I renounce all part in you: no such hands
> As yours will have my soul. I'll burn it
> Away like the city, I'll hurt you
> In the centre of your love, as you do me
> (3:265)

Finally he has to admit defeat, first before his own body and then before God, to whom he concedes victory: "There's no argument any more, and no more heavy blows between us" (3:275). Henry has Roger call back the monk who has just cursed him to administer absolution and benediction, which the monk, by his vows, the laws of his calling, will be obliged to do. Henry emphasizes the underlying importance of laws in all areas so that people can live and die according to perceived needs: "The formalities of allegiance. I believe in the law" (3:275). The implication is that God also will accept Henry's return to him, his defiance over. King's law and God's law converge at this final moment.

Becket's first-act philosophical speech on law and grace begins with a discussion of experience:

> What a man knows he has by experience,
> But what a man is precedes experience.
> His experience merely reveals him, or destroys him;
> Either drives him to his own negation,
> Or persuades him to his affirmation, as he chooses.
>   (3:218)

The essence is already given, and all subsequent life has to work on that material; it cannot deny or ignore the original essence of being. Fry said that Becket "was speaking for me there" in voicing this belief in the first, given ground plan of character.[1] Henry's experience in the play both reveals and destroys him, and he dies a flawed, admirable, pathetic figure, his sons' hostility balanced by Roger's and William Marshal's devotion.

Becket is a more enigmatic figure. There are several plays about Becket, and Fry was concerned to focus on Henry and avoid repeating other writers' material, especially *Murder in the Cathedral*. Becket's complexities are sketched in act 1. As chancellor he has apparently been as spectacular a success as he was as a soldier. On the battlefield, he "stacks the countryside with Christian / Corpses" (3:191), and as a diplomat he crosses France in a "procession of the mad world . . . a holy menagerie / Of opulence and power" (3:191) while remaining "an incorruptible virgin," to which Henry adds, "Your virginity's / As crass extravagant as the rest of your ways of living" (3:191). He flings himself into being an archbishop with similar thoroughness, as revealed by the clerk's testimony to "how utterly he has put aside all ostentation; how he feasts the poor, visits the sick, and every day washes the feet of thirteen beggars" (3:208). This brings a wry comment form Henry on such lack of "ostentation": "A very sagacious and elaborate performance. I hope the beggars are well paid" (3:208). These performances, suggesting self-dramatization, show an element of insecurity; Becket needs his audience to exist, as he says himself:

> What I do well
> I do because men believe I will do it well
> Before ever the thing is begun . . .
> . . . I care for men's opinion.
> I doubt if I should ever be
> Sufficient in myself, to hold my course
> Without any approval. No one would say
> I was made of the stuff of martyrs.
>
> (3:198)

Offstage in Canterbury, Becket is struggling to become what he seems. His reliance on approval appears in his wavering during the court scene in act 2: refusing, agreeing, then again refusing obedience to the king. Fry remarked of his subject, "I couldn't understand why it was Becket, and not Henry, who had had the plays written about him. I came to understand later!" ("Talking of Henry," 186). Becket's behavior is contradictory and complex, implying that his motives are complex too, an interesting situation for writer and audience. Fry, however, saw Henry's single-mindedness as causing him greater suffering: "It was the degree of self-deception in Becket's thrust and the whole anguish of Henry's parry; so that I was driven to ask myself whether, by his dedicated suffering for an ideal (his Passion, in a religious sense), Henry was not the more saintly of the two."[2]

In *Curtmantle* we hear Becket's early self-explanation, and his later defense of the church's position, but after his trial, his motives become darker. Why does he flee to France rather than pursue his struggle with Henry? Why does he agree to be reconciled with him and then challenge him with excommunication and aggression from his followers? The marshal suggests: "Thinking back on it now, he seemed to me like a man / Who had gone through life saving up all passion / To spend at last on his own downfall" (3:248). Possibly Becket was at last responding to the divine expectations focused on his role as archbishop rather than to human expectations.

But we have only the surmises of the other characters, and this marginalization of Becket toward the end, in contrast to his earlier stance as mighty opposite to Henry, contributes to the faltering development of act 2 with its long series of different problems, met and disposed of by Henry. The opening duel between the two men causes suspense as to how this conflict will unfold, and it seems that there was no need to tone down Becket so as to prevent his rivaling Henry. Essentially Henry needs antagonists to show his self-willed nature.

In the first production, Alan Dobie's performance as Becket came in for some criticism as being disappointing—not enough of the saint and martyr that the audience was expecting. Bamber Gascoigne in the *Spectator*, however, thought "the waspishly dry way in which Alan Dobie plays Becket ends up by being entirely convincing," though whether this brought out the extravagance or the insecurity Fry intended seems doubtful.[3] And while critics liked the beginning and end of the play—"a magnificent first act" (*Spectator*) [4] and "the last splendidly theatrical scene outside the blazing town" (*Illustrated London News*)[5]—some felt that the second act conflict was not successful and lacked dramatic tension. Harold Hobson, however, singled out the Henry-Becket debates as "muscled, dramatic, probing," though he thought the other episodes were less effective.[6] Gascoigne also picked out the end of act 2 as particularly successful in its staging: "It is set in autumnal colours of brown and gold on a splendid abstract stage by Abd' Elkader Farrah, made up of sloping platforms and looking like a large flat-backed crab with its tail in the air and one claw raised towards the audience . . . there are four vast knights ranged along the crab's tail, quietly and ominously waiting."[7]

Perhaps the fixed order of the historical events undermined the dramatic order in act 2 in that the deadlock of the trial is followed by Henry's other conflict with Eleanor and the jealous sons, while Becket disappears into exile, whereas the dramatic structure would be tighter if the Becket story could have been unhistorically sustained and telescoped to reach its climax before the family conflicts started. But Fry was convinced that by electing to write a genuinely historical play, he must follow the historical chronology "without distorting the material he has chosen to use. Otherwise let him invent his characters, let him go to Ruritania for his history" (3:173). He later added: "How much historical fact can be distorted for the sake of theatrical effectiveness is a matter of the playwright's conscience. I believe that keeping faith with the past is more important than the dividends to be got from unjustified flashes of 'good theatre'" ("Theatre and History," 87). Important though the conflict with Becket was, Henry's life contained far more elements of interest.

Because of the concentration of action around Henry, on stage for almost the whole play, Eleanor is reduced to a supporting role, though this in itself is significant in showing her frustration at Henry's neglect. She says, "Now I m nothing in this land" (3:231), and tells Becket:

> But I see
> The only way I can have any part in life
> Is to stand and be the curious onlooker
> While two unproved worlds fly at each other.
> (3:216)

Personally she resents Henry's unfaithfulness; she who has been, as Henry himself says, "the haunter of male imagination / Ever since I could understand sex" (3:194), is neglected for all his other mistresses. His preference for "Fair Rosamund" is particularly galling because it is public knowledge. Similarly she is angry that he ignores her political and intellectual abilities, brought up as she has been in the traditions of hereditary rulers, "a race of men / Born to act on events like sun on the vine" (3:231). Though a woman, she asserts her inheritance of power and influence, and when Henry claims, "Your true reality / Is in guarding what I have made," she retorts, "It's in myself, past, present and to come" (3:239). This is not so much a declaration of her rights as a wife or as a royal queen but a reminder that each individual's true reality must be developed on its own terms, not forced into another's mold.

Eleanor puts forward the central theme of tolerance and difference, and she repeatedly reminds us of the strangeness and unpredictability of life—in opposition to Henry's assertion of system and control. Henry ignores her central speech in act 2 when she appeals to him:

> Consider complexity, delight in difference.
> Fear, for God's sake, your exact words.
> Do you think you can draw lines on the living water?
> Together we might make a world of progress.
> Between us, by our three variants of human nature,
> You and Becket and me, we could be
> The complete reaching forward.
> (3:226)

Henry goes on as if she had not spoken—she says, "You saw, Marshal, how he turned away from me?"—but Eleanor represents here an important third way: if all human beings need an adversarial system of church and state to cater to their conflicting spiritual and physical needs, perhaps they also need a mediating spirit of tolerance to break out of this simple dialectic and carry humanity on to the true progress proposed in *A Sleep of Prisoners*. Eleanor later says, "God thrives on chance and change" (3:260), because this is how humanity gradually moves beyond the limited vision of its leaders. Henry's selfish dominance is evident in his lack of concern for Eleanor, but her suggestions also highlight the limitations of his legal system.

In *Curtmantle* only Henry's four sons appear (historically he had two daughters as well), and the conventional antagonism of fathers and sons undermines their relationship. Henry's gift of responsibility to his sons, supposedly to establish them in their places early in life, is only an illusion. Harry is kept in prolonged dependence, "never given the powers that belong to me" (3:258), and Richard and Geoffrey seem independent only because they escape to a different country. Harry's deferred kingship still creates jealousy among the others, as does Henry's favoritism toward the youngest, John. Overbearing though Henry is, the sons' defiance of him is not attractive. Harry is weak and complaining, Richard aggressive and callous, Geoffrey self-centered, and John cunning and self-seeking. Richard particularly shows little sign of his heroic historical image as the Lionheart; he turns Henry's complaints of their attitude back on himself: "You can't rob us of your nature (3:261). And at Henry's last pathetic fall at his defeat at Le Mans, where even Philip of France offers gentleness, Richard intervenes with, "He's playing for pity" (3:269), and walks away without a backward glance at the fallen king. Audience sympathy, alienated perhaps by Henry's rejection of Becket or his crude arrest of Eleanor, swings back to him when he is compared with his unheroic sons.

Henry's fifth son, the illegitimate Roger, plays a significant role as the only loyal and loving member of his family. Roger has no rights and no supporters and is uncorrupted by jealousy and greed; ironically, it is the illegitimate son who thinks more of obligations than of claims. "I owe you a life, sir" (3:273), he says to the dying king; in justice, the legitimate sons should owe him much more. It is evidence of the rule of chance and change rather than of justice that Roger has unexpectedly turned out to be the truest son to Henry.

In his article on the play, Fry particularly stressed the importance of verse in expressing the inner nature of a character: "Anyway I need to use verse when a speech has to become—how shall I say?—like an object reflecting that inner shaping of the character, that process of evolution" ("Talking of Henry," 87). Something of this is evident in the speech styles of Henry and Becket. Henry characteristically speaks in simple statements and questions and uses the more common complex sentences, as in :

> All right, you confer the favour. I thought that I did.
> But what difference? We shall go ahead.
> Make away with your uncertainties, man.

> Anything unaccustomed has a doubtful look
> Till it grows to be a part of our thinking.
>
> (3:201)

The confidence and the habit of command are evident behind his style—no need to persuade or concede or qualify. Becket, on the other hand, expresses his insecurity. Even as the spokesman of the absolute, he knows the dangers and vulnerability of his position more thoroughly than Henry ever does. He rejects the supremacy of the king firmly but at once goes on to express the complication of the human situation in a series of repetitive concessions that remind us of earlier Eliotian influence:

> Nothing. Nothing from the King. Whatever the Church
> Holds is held in perpetual liberty.
> I am your father, though you hold me in disdain:
> Still and always your father, however vexed in thought,
> Fallible in action, unpersuading in word,
> Falling short in everything that makes
> A man convince his times with truth. In spite
> Of all, your father; and by a father's authority
> I forbid you to give sentence.
>
> (3:228)

Later, however, as Henry's optimism falters and the inner shaping and evolution move toward embitterment, his sentences, though still tending to be simply accumulative, include more amplification. The crisp, regal assertion of will is no longer enough as he realizes he may inadvertently have ordered Becket's murder:

> Dear Christ, the day that any man would dread
> Is when life goes separate from the man,
> When he speaks what he doesn't say, and does
> What is not his doing, and an hour of the day
> Which was unimportant as it went by
> Comes back revealed as the satan of all hours,
> Which will never let the man go.
>
> (3:250–51)

Curtmantle follows the stylistic development of *Dark* toward less imagery and less wordplay, and of those unobtrusive images that do occur throughout the dialogue, many relate to nature, particularly climate and weather, although most of the action takes place in castle and palace. Nature invades the palace in the visual form of a bewildering fog that pours across the uncomprehending confrontation of church and state. Eleanor sees the London streets as chilling in their hostility, her exile a punishment "for loving life too warmly" (3:215), and she makes her court at Poitou a place of "warm sun" metaphorically as well as literally. Henry hopes for change in fortune with a change in the weather: "Do you see / The bated look the sky has? The way of the wind / Is altering. The trees are drawn with chalk on slate," but "the morning was only another day. It emerged sullen and bedraggled, after a night of bucketing rain" (3:233). The characters seem to appeal to nature from a position of unnatural constraint. Only Becket looks beneath the surface to the patterns shown by nature—echoing Merlin in *Thor*, paradoxically, Merlin being scoffed at twice in this play—and sees God's purpose there: "In the avalanche of snow / The star figure of the flake is there unchanged. / It was out of a whirlwind that God answered Job" (3:219).

The concept of a deeper pattern, which humanity may or may not perceive, also underlies Eleanor's use of one of the rare music images in the play:

> Here he will find the laws
> Keep time in him like his own heart; for here
> We govern as music governs itself within,
> By the silent order whose speech is all visible things.
>   (3:256)

On the other hand, songs lead to dissent in the royal household, in both the case of Eleanor's reference to the popular tune about Henry's mistress, "that Welsh harp, Rosamund de Clifford" (3:232), its popularity constantly reminding her of her rival, and the fight between Harry and Richard provoked by Richard's mocking song; evidently his talents as a minstrel do not lead to harmony.

Disharmony pervades *Curtmantle*. Images of violence and blood run through the play, from Eleanor's half-joking comparison of the debate to a bullfight—"Be sure you draw blood, to lift my dropping spirits" (3:216), and "Who has left most blood on the sand, Marshal?" (3:226)—to the disastrous last campaign through towns whose streets "were like furrows, or scars, rather" (3:263). This is part of Henry's heritage: "I had a demon for an ancestor. / There are times I feel her wading in my blood and howling /

For a sacrifice of obscurantical fools" (3:220). Another bloodthirsty outburst like this leads to the assassination of Becket. Becket himself is the pretext for his followers' violence, and Foliot says that he "cuts us out of the Church's body like tumours" (3:249). As Foliot had rightly warned, there is a fatal absolutism in Becket, equal to Henry's violence, as appears when he arrives carrying his own cross "like drawing a sword out of the scabbard in the King's face" (3:227).

In a wider sense, blood focuses attention on the human complexity with which Henry was wrestling as he tried to impose his will on the kingdom. Blood reminds us of the common humanity of the characters. Beneath the great issues contending are men of flesh and blood, and Roger, trying to part the fighting princes, protests that they are spilling "my blood too . . . the blood of the whole body / Of Plantagenet government" (3:242). Blood both unites and divides the Plantagenets, as it does the loyal, contentious, religious, ungrateful citizens of England.

Henry is perhaps the most tragic of Fry's warrior figures. Moses in *The Firstborn* and Cymen in *Thor* can look forward to the achievement of a new order in spite of the sacrifices they have made; but Henry has always pushed the demands of blood, his own or others, into situations of conflict that are harmful rather than productive. And yet he has a true vision of peace and protection for the weak, which his own conflicts make harder to achieve. Being only a man of flesh and blood, he cannot separate the energy needed to accomplish his vision from the impulsive violence that crushes enemy and friend alike. He dies "in great anxiety," saying, "I don't know . . . if the laws will hold . . . It is all still to do!" (3:275).

Chapter Ten
Two Folktales in *A Yard of Sun*

The germ of *A Yard of Sun* came from the same source as *Lady*, the collection of German stories.[1] The story has a typical folktale outline: a good man has three sons and offers each a share of his savings to seek their fortune with. The youngest son is, as usual, an exception and decides to become a thief. This family conflict is moved from the folklorique past and set precisely in July 1946, in a Siena just recovering from the war, with shortages, returning soldiers and prisoners, hostility, grief, guilt, and recrimination. The three sons of Angelino Bruno made their choices before the war. Roberto, the eldest, trained as a doctor; he treats only the poor, for little or no payment. Luigi has tried to become a politician, and because he chose the losing side by joining the fascist party, he is now defeated and unprosperous. The youngest son, Edmondo, the prospective thief, is never mentioned. When Angelino in outrage had withheld both blessing and money, Edmondo blackmailed an equivalent sum from an old neighbor and disappeared to pursue his chosen career. Angelino himself is caretaker of the empty Palazzo Traguardo and runs a small osteria, or café. When the play opens, we see the continuous bickering between the two elder brothers. Roberto, a violent idealist, has been a communist patriot partisan during the war, fighting guerrilla skirmishes against the German and fascist forces. Luigi seems to have joined the fascists through opportunism and thoughtlessness rather than conviction, but his refusal to see this as any more serious than a mistake drives Roberto to fury.

Angelino trots back and forth trying to keep the peace between them. His good nature hovers over the courtyard of the Palazzo, where all the action takes place, and which is the yard of sun of the title. He would agree with Luigi that it is time to forget the past and look hopefully to the future. The most important prospect is that his miserable income from caretaking will increase because new, rich owners of the Palazzo are about to arrive; moreover, for the first time since the war, Siena is about to put on the Palio, a horse race in the town square, each horse representing a parish of the town, accompanied by processions and pageantry, participants dressed in Renaissance cos-

tume, banners, trumpeters, and general festivity. As Luigi says, there is hope
of a new start and a return to the good old days.

First, however, the subplot is introduced. At the other side of the courtyard
from Angelino's osteria is the apartment of nineteen-year-old Grazia, who
lives with her mother, Giosetta, and whose father, Cesare, captured as a deserter by the SS three years previously, has never been heard of since. Grazia
passes through the courtyard introducing Alfio, who has been asking the way
and is now revealed to be the son of Cesare's legitimate wife back in Naples,
whom he had deserted before he met Giosetta. By coincidence, he is also the
jockey hired by a rival parish to ride in the Palio. An innocent, well-meaning
young man, Alfio presents a threat to the well-being of the neighborhood in
two ways. But as Giosetta (who knows the whole story) and Grazia meet and
accept him and as the Brunos are confident of the superiority of their parish's
famous and brilliant rider, this threat seems to fade. The wrangling of the
brothers takes the foreground again, and they are actually fighting when
Ana-Clara, wife of the new owner, appears. Roberto's embarrassment increases his ideological hostility to this rich, beautiful, rather mysterious young
foreigner (Ana-Clara is Portuguese), and she is left to fascinate Luigi and
Angelo, making a dazzling impression before her husband arrives.

The climax of this stage of the plot comes with the appearance of this new
owner, who turns out to be Edmondo, the youngest son. "Thief" was evidently a shorthand term for "ruthless and successful businessman," and he
has returned, triumphant and rich, to shower wealth on his family. Although
this is the climax of the folk story, it is only the beginning of the main action
of this play. Edmondo, though sincere in his wish to make everyone happy,
effectively begins another folktale by taking on the role of tempter toward his
family and friends. One of the main plot lines is the question of which neighborhood will win the Palio, for the honor, glory, and money wagered on it.
Edmondo has intervened by hiring Cambriccio, a nationally famous (and expensive) star jockey, giving his parish an advantage far beyond the usual fair
competition. And mainly because of Roberto's suspicions about the probable
profiteering and exploitation that has made Edmondo's fortune while the
rest of them have been suffering during the war, the other characters are not
able to rejoice quite wholeheartedly in the unfair advantage Edmondo has
bought them. The atmosphere develops tension and resentment instead of
jollity.

As the second act unfolds, we see how Edmondo's gifts and offers tempt
the characters not only to an easy materialism but to an indulgence of their
own weaknesses. Luigi wants to imitate and hang on to Edmondo to take a
shortcut to politics and power. Grazia, at first merely amused by her trial ses

sion as a fashion model, wants to leave her home and plunge into smart Roman society as an escape from her sense of guilt. She fears secretly that it was her incautious words to a friend that betrayed her father to the Nazis, and she cannot face or come to terms with this possibility. When Cambriccio, the jockey, has an accident, Edmondo bribes Alfio to ride badly and lose the race for his employers; the indignant Alfio eventually agrees because his invalid mother needs expensive American drugs. Angelino's dream of presiding over a large but exclusive restaurant is offered him as a gift, with no effort required from himself. And though this is not Edmondo's intention, the beauty and apparently aristocratic superiority of Ana-Clara tempt Roberto to try to seduce her and lower both her pride and the triumph of his young brother. As she points out, this is the same kind of destructive manipulation of other people that he condemns in his enemies.

The turning point of this strange mixture of hope and anxiety is triggered by Grazia's sudden confession of her conviction of guilt. Roberto's better side revives to comfort her, and he begins to realize he loves Grazia, not Ana-Clara. Giosetta tells her that an anonymous note received that morning claimed that Cesare is alive and presumably on his way home. Reunion with Cesare puts all thoughts of escape through fashion modeling out of Grazia's head, and the appearance of Cesare reverses Alfio's acceptance of the bribe. He cannot cheat with his father watching the race. Ana-Clara and Roberto agree to forget the real attraction that had begun between them and remain friends. Gradually all the ill effects of Edmondo's temptations begin to fade.

There is no formal scene division, but a short interval of darkness, with sound effects to suggest that the Palio is taking place, carries the action to the following afternoon. Cesare and Giosetta are the only ones who have not gone to watch the Palio, and when Grazia returns with Roberto, Cesare tells them that he has decided to return to his wife, Alfio's mother, to ease her last weeks of dying. Another surprise is that although Luigi had been the only available rider and fell off after a circuit and a half, their parish horse has won the Palio, because the Palio rule is that "if the horse comes in, the race is won, / Never mind what happens to the man."[2] Luigi no longer needs Edmondo now that he has made a name for himself by his own efforts. Even Angelino finds he does not want his restaurant when it is offered to him. He speaks for all the characters who have preferred their own individual concerns to the temptations of realized fantasies: "I like to enjoy / A glittering prospect, but not to the extent / Of letting it take you over body and soul" (108). Edmondo leaves as he had come, with his train of servants, baggage, car, and wife, discomfited but unchanged. The inhabitants of the yard of sun have reformed their lives without him—Roberto has decided to marry Grazia, and

Alfio has become part of his stepfamily—but Ana-Clara's promise of reunion on "some other evening" suggests a less strained, more equal relationship of reconciliation in the future.

Coincidentally this play from the same source as *Lady* has a similar distribution of characters among the generations and sexes: several young men, two young women, an older woman, and two older men. The practical result is the same atmosphere of multiple activity and intrigue as the young men come into conflict among themselves and the plot relationships develop among the characters. Thematically, however, *A Yard of Sun* has surprisingly much in common with the apparently dissimilar *A Sleep of Prisoners*. Set just after World War II, *Yard*, like *Sleep*, is preoccupied with issues of aggression, commitment, and forgiveness. Roberto is as violent as Dave King, as we see in his Cain and Abel struggle with his brother, Luigi, where Luigi, "frightened," cries, "Do you want to kill me?" (28). His reaction to Edmondo's "modeling" plans for Grazia is, "I could kill Edmondo" (60). And later, when Edmondo, nettled by his criticism, refers to blood guiltiness, Roberto grabs him across the table, shouting, "I'll kill you!" (77)

Yet as in Dave's King David dream in *Sleep*, the aggressiveness is only a way of showing concern and even love; "why won't they see? I care what they think and do, my bloody family" (50). His other roles, as a doctor and a political idealist, seem ridiculously incongruous with his destructive impulses and demonstrate his pattern of conflicting values. The beneficent aspect of Roberto's profession shows the caring side of human nature. With his patients he is, as Ana-Clara describes,

> . . . generous . . . and human—the very
> Charm in you that does them good . . .
> . . . You came
> Far nearer to prodding my social conscience awake
> By letting me see they loved you, than with all
> That rhapsody of statistics.
>
> (61)

Its other aspect is a materialism that appears also in his politics; everything is reduced to material cause and effect. He is more interested, at least on a conscious level, in the physical hardship of his patients and the economic influences on their poor health than in the human comfort he brings them. Similarly he blames the local government for the failure of the water supply during flooding that afflicts the town for the duration of the play—"You see / The hopeless way this town is organized!" (2)—a view countered by

Angelino's explanation that the council is hardly responsible for the emergency of the flood: "That's an Act of God / Not a political manifesto" (2). But Roberto does not admit anything other than material needs and influences: "If we get the conditions straight, the rest will follow" (103), he tells Cesare, echoing the systematic narrowness of King Henry in *Curtmantle*.

Roberto's practical view of human life is related to Edmondo's even narrower materialism, which ironically Roberto angrily rejects:

> And you think you can bring your filthy money here
> And buy us over again into the old
> Discredited welter of greeds we've just been fighting
> Our way out of.
>
> (78)

Roberto also thinks that money is essential to the improvement of life but wants it to be fairly and objectively applied to the needs of the community, while Edmondo is interested only in what his money can do for himself and those he personally is concerned with—and there is evidently a strong recognition of the power that money confers.

Edmondo is generally indifferent to any nonmaterial values. He calls himself "an internationalist, the same as any / Reasonable business man" (44). Obviously "internationalist" to him has not the positive meaning of supporting human brotherhood but the negative sense of rejecting any ties or loyalties or commitment. Like Peter-Absalom as seen by Dave in *Sleep,* Edmondo pretends that everything is tolerable, nothing is to be condemned. Edmondo's social detachment is as questionable as Roberto's violence. As in *Dark* and *Sleep*, evil needs resisting, though not with too-ready violence, and profiteering from a war is not resistance to evil. The inadequacy of Edmondo's approach is established straightaway when he proclaims himself ready to repay the neighbor whose savings he had blackmailed from him many years ago, only to hear that "he died last night," and his attempt to compensate for this—"his son must have it"—is also foiled: "Mario was killed" (45–46). The rest of the play goes on to demonstrate that the characters have other values more important to them than what Edmondo's money can buy.

One of the most eager to accept Edmondo's gifts, and to follow in his footsteps, Luigi is a character who shows how even the most unpromising human material has hopes of redemption and improvement. His repentance for his fascist past is not intense enough to satisfy Roberto, but he is eternally hopeful, not only in that he has an optimistic personality but in that he represents the potential goodness and spiritual development of every person.

Others may have low expectations of him—"I know what you mean, though. I haven't ever brought anything off yet" (72), he admits—and he feels with some justification that Roberto is hindering him from forgetting his "false start":

> You are an unforgiving
> Unfair bastard! Why am I supposed
> To be the particularly guilty one?
> Because eight years ago I put on a dirty shirt.
>
> (8)

This develops into a debate between them:

> Is a man never to be allowed to grow
> Out of the compost of his own mistakes
> And be accepted on his present showing?
>
> (12)

opposed by Roberto's mistrust:

> You haven't convinced me that anything has altered.
> You seem to think that every change of wind
> That crosses your mind is a kind of baptism.
>
> (12)

Predictably, Luigi claims that the Palio symbolically "hymns our power of survival over oppression, / Defeat and death" (32), and his qualified triumph in the race confirms the possibility of growth and reformation.

It is, however, Cesare who exemplifies most clearly the religious theme of guilt, reparation, and redemption, as well as suggesting a better future for the whole of humanity. Giosetta tells Angelino how Cesare's marriage to Alfio's mother had been a torment for both of them. Her illness had seemed at first "hardly more than a fear of being made love to. / He got it in his head that he was crucifying her, / And hated the life in his own body" (56). His guilt stays with him like a sense of original sin, and though happy with Giosetta, he often plunged into misery and bouts of drinking, questioning his conscience: "Had he run from what God wanted of him?" (56). This is why he resolves, after the joyful reunion with Giosetta and Grazia, to go back to his wife who, Alfio has explained, is dying: "easing the sting of death in the next bunk / Is something I know about" (100). Alfio goes through a simila though much briefer, torment when he wavers about accepting the bribe to lose the race—accepting it first as the lesser of two evils and then deciding to do the right thing.

Guilt can be productive or counterproductive. Cesare's guilt prompts him to dedicate himself to making his wife's last days more comfortable (and because Giosetta has the prospect of his later return, the sufferings of his second family do not outweigh the benefits of his decision). Grazia's secret guilt at having told of Cesare's hiding place, however, is merely damaging. Roberto says: "I could have told you; once you had blamed yourself / You let fear take substance, and become / An ogre of certainty, who was never there" (84). Grazia's responsibility for Cesare's capture is not certain, and the friend she confided in may or may not have mentioned the secret, again unintentionally. Thus the fault here is, at least to Roberto, less culpable than Luigi's thoughtless fascism. Yet in both cases the action of the play shows that new bright beginnings and forgiveness are possible. Grazia regains her cheerfulness with Roberto's sympathy and Cesare's return; Luigi rises to the occasion of riding bareback to save the district; and Cesare expresses the possibility of forgiveness by refusing to become embittered by his experience in the prison camp. As Roberto says, "God knows you've got every reason to feel / The human experiment has failed," but Cesare replies, "I never set / So much value on us as I do now" (103). He rejects vindictiveness and despair and cries: "Purify us, Roberto, purify us! / Insist on all the powers that recover us!" (104).

Because of his years in the prison camp, Cesare has, as Ana-Clara notices, come to perceive another reality in human life. Like Meadows at the end of *Sleep*, he urges a new vision of the others—"the real revolution, / The transformation" (103). It is a spiritual and mental transformation that he wants, and he challenges Edmondo's and Roberto's materialistic ideas of progress:

> I was wondering
> Just what state of mind gives us a future.
> I suppose you mean the future; not the present
> Made more bearable or more efficient.
> What's the good if it's not a difference in kind? . . .
> . . . Where does the mind go next, in your well-cared-for
> System of being born and being buried?
> I haven't your simple faith that man can be doctored
> Out of his tragedy into the millennium.
>
>   (103)

Human life is potentially a tragedy, not a simple problem to be solved by money or social administration. Unexpectedly, Ana-Clara is another character who perceives this possibility of transformation, and she suggests that all experience may be provisional or indeterminate in definition: "There may always be another reality / To make fiction of the truth we think we've arrived at" (93). The exaltation of the Palio brings her the promise of such a transformation: "All through the afternoon / I felt as though the barriers were breaking / Between our world and another" (107). The atmosphere of the Palio gave hints of what a higher state of being could be like:

> So nearly the city had no need of the sun
> Or the moon to shine on it. I could almost see
> By the light that streamed from the trumpets
> And shimmered from the bell. The courting sun-birds,
> The birds of paradise, so nearly sang
> The indwelling music that created us.
>
> (107)

"Nearly . . . almost . . . nearly": this higher state has to be achieved by a change of heart and of values, only faintly shadowed in the communal celebrations of the Palio.[3] As in some of the other plays, there are references to an underlying force aiding the movement of humanity toward this spiritual development, a force that is the dynamic aspect of God's purpose for humanity. Fry wrote, "We are all involved in a process which it is simpler to call God than anything else, and if I can manage to write about—not theories—but what it feels like to be a living man in fact I am writing about what every man feels, even if in doubt or rejection" ("Talking of Henry," 189). Cesare and Ana-Clara consciously feel the process that is God's pressure toward development, and the others manifest it less consciously in their acts of affection and benevolence, however tainted by self-interest. Here the process is referred to as life—the course of events through which human beings are carried along toward fulfillment of God's purpose. Luigi complains to Roberto, "You won't / Allow that life ever knows her own business" (6), and triumphantly reasserts after his victory, "How was that, Bobo? I just gave life a chance / To find her own way" (105). Roberto admits that there is a hidden direction to life: "I suppose life is willing, when we can find / What it's groping for" (67). As we have seen, this is the effect of the play as a whole: things right themselves.

It will be clear from this discussion of the conflicting values in the play that, again as in *Lady*, the characters have a representative function: Roberto standing for idealistic violence, Edmondo for money, Luigi for opportunism, Cesare for redemption, and so on. In most cases the characters are evidently more complex than the single value label indicates. Luigi perhaps is a shallow character, but nonetheless he swings convincingly between bumptiousness and humility, self-assertion and nervousness. Ironically Grazia's innocence, which is what she means for Roberto—"The best one of all of us, / Who has lived these years without a mark against her" (78)—conceals her own guilty self-condemnation. Roberto particularly mingles social self-righteousness with the spontaneous human affection Ana-Clara notices, and though Luigi criticizes his extremism—"You're always either killing or curing" (6)—he is no callous fanatic but responds to suffering personally, not only that of his patients but also Grazia's. Both Roberto and Luigi can forget their differences and behave like brothers again when they unite in teasing Alfio.

Ana-Clara too has a complex character. She represents the power of love but is concerned with her own individual development. Apparently a *"donnanobile"* (noble lady; 94), she eventually confesses, provoked by Roberto's scolding, that she was born in a slum and as a child "was a better beggar than all the nuns / Of Portugal" (65). But she also claims that "that squalid childhood / Lied about every living thing that was in me" (65). There is a hint here of the philosophy expounded by Becket in *Curtmantle*—that "what a man is precedes experience" (3:218); his innate character or potential is only confirmed or damaged—not originated—by his life experiences. Ana-Clara has preserved her innate life through the damaging experience of squalor until at fifteen she precociously took a lover, a young actor, who helped her to escape from the effects of squalor, not with money but by love and education: "He was like a redeemer / Piercing the darkness for me" (66). Two years of hopeful learning from him how to become an actress have equipped her to pass as a *donnanobile* outwardly, and her next lover, a university lecturer, continued the education of the inner woman with poetry, philosophy, and music. When he left, she met Edmondo, who has little to teach her but offers a free partnership within which she can develop herself:

> This time I could love from a level start.
> He and I were climbing the same pitch . . .
> . . . And now no matter how far I stretched my arms
> No walls were there, nothing to frown on me.
>
> (67)

Paradoxically, Edmondo's lack of convictions is liberating in the freedom it allows her. Her life, then, has been an onward progress of self-discovery and development, and therefore she is prepared to understand Cesare's idea of a transformation. It is, she realizes, "as if / Our variation to adapt to life / Was hardly begun" (107).

The brief feeling of love between Ana-Clara and Roberto is, however, a false trail; his wish for a better future is still narrowly social and material, and his proselytizing enthusiasm is oppressive. He, on the other hand, may have learned to be more tolerant, and his prospective marriage to Grazia and continued friendship with Ana-Clara, his sister-in-law, will no doubt affect him further. *Yard* thus joins the majority of the soldier and lady plays in which the soldier is affected more than the lady. In Ana-Clara's short account of her life, love has been a tributary to her own development, not a means of exploitation, and her vision of the Palio gives it a double symbolism—as "a great slow love-making" (107) and as a representation of a spiritually elevated and unified state of being. During the play, she too has developed from having a pragmatic, sexually based assessment of people and circumstances to an appreciation of human value and possible spiritual significance.

The Palio has a practical function as pretext for several of the plot complications; it also is one of the most important symbols through which the philosophical and religious significance of the action is expressed. *Sleep* had the overt parables of the biblical dreams and Meadows's explicit exhortation at the end; the characters in *Dark* include a group of variously philosophical and articulate people, who made the issues that arise in it equally explicit. *Yard*, however, is more firmly secular in its situation. The discussions that arise are ethical and social rather than religious, and the spiritual dimension has to be implied by symbolic means, at least until Cesare appears as its spokesman toward the end.

Luigi describes the origins of the Palio, centuries earlier, after a savage siege in which two-thirds of the inhabitants of Siena had starved to death and the remnant had ignominiously given up the town. The Palio and its procession had been instituted to reassert civic pride—"Pride in our flair for resurrection" (32). Luigi shows by his own comic triumph that there is hope of renewal after error and shame; the background to the action is the gradual revival of a country recovering from defeat. Cesare, like other surviving prisoners, has been resurrected from a place of death and has become transfigured, bringing a message of hope and love. The experience of the Palio, which Ana-Clara compares to a transition into another world, derives its force partly from the intense sense of unity and participation among all present. Fry added as an appendix to the published text a note written by Stewart Perowne for the *Times* describing the pageantry of the procession in great detail and stressing its almost mystic intensity:

The remarkable thing about the display is its complete naturalness. These lads (few are over thirty) are not players: they are, not act, what we see. There is not a whiff of Wardour Street about it. Here for a day the Middle Ages has become *primavera,* first youth. . . . Only the horses and riders are there for the spectators, who by their emotion become fused into participation.

To participate, to belong, to be. If anything is still left remarkable beneath the visited moon, here it is man himself, who in Siena can still surpass, in appeal and impact, the most splendid shadows of Verona's operas. (112–13)

Both aspects of the Palio are echoed in music images, as so often in Fry's other plays. Luigi's first appearance is heralded by his "mongrel tenor," which he defends as "my part in the song of praise. If we're not equipped / To give thanks we shouldn't give up trying" (5). His readiness to renew himself appears in this faulty but willing song. Ana-Clara's reference to the Palio as "so nearly" reproducing "the indwelling music that created us" (107) expresses Fry's recurrent idea of an underlying pattern, God's purpose for the next stage of humanity's development, reflected in the laws and beauty of musical form.

The great virtue of the inhabitants of the sunlit yard is their human love, symbolized by the emblem of their parish, the pelican, which according to myth lovingly fed its young on its own lifeblood. The temptations of selfishness that seek to undermine this love, set in motion by Edmondo's return, coincide with the failure of the water supply. Roberto's narrow ideology makes him want to withhold the emergency provision of water from the Palazzo's new owners, while Giosetta's unselfish love is shown in her decision to share her water churn with the unknown newcomers. As Edmondo's offerings fail—as Alfio decides to reject the bribe, as Ana-Clara reasserts her loyalty to her husband, as Grazia forgets her wish to escape from home and guilt, and as Cesare returns—the renewed flow of love and unselfish values is signaled by the reestablishment of the water supply (which is red like the pelican's blood): "There's water in the taps, / Did you know? Arterial red, like the Tiber. / I'll leave it running and see if it comes clear" (96).

As these speeches suggest, the language of *Yard* is fuller of imagery of all kinds than *Dark* or *Curtmantle.* On the other hand, the characters are more restrained in their uses of imagery and wordplay than those of *Lady* or *Venus.* Though less inventive in his vocabulary, Angelino perhaps has a little of Reedbeck about him, both in his cheerfulness and his imaginative readiness with images and similarities. He makes a long speech to describe Cesare's probable methods of keeping his memory of Giosetta alive:

> like any other
> Marooned man who has to improvise
> His woman out of a desert, out of a breathing
> Cinder from the stove, or holding his boot
> In his hands as he used to hold your face, anything
> (55)

Giosetta underlines its deliberate extravagance by replying, "Trust you to make an opera out of it. / I'm bothered enough, without having to be / Madam Butterfly with the boot face" (55). On a larger scale, Ana-Clara's description of the Palio, using prolonged and consistent sexual imagery, is a conscious set piece:

> The Commune flag fluttering, while the Commune bell
> Jerks in the erect campanile,
> Like an alarm, and like a gloria; both.
> And all the time the banners ripple and leap,
> Circle the body, stroke and rouse
> With creating hands. Oh, it really is, you know,
> A lovemaking, a fishing in sensitive pools . . .
> . . . At last when the corporate body has been tautened
> Absolutely to expectation's limit
> There comes the violent release, the orgasm,
> The animal explosion of the horse race,
> Bare-backed and savage.
> (33)

But these are exceptions; the images on the whole appear regularly but at intervals—something like one in a short speech, three on different subjects in a long speech. Edmondo, for instance, resents his father and brothers with one vivid image in a speech of otherwise brief clichés:

> I give up!
> I might have known it was no good trying to get
> This bunkered family on to the fairway. Do
> What you like with him. Chuck the race away,
> If that's what you want. Don't come crying to me.
> (89)

A Yard of Son was provisionally titled *The Heat of the Day,* but Fry chose the final title to make a slight pun on *yard* as the courtyard of its setting and as the measurement, a yard as only a small amount of sunlight for each person. It was produced at the Nottingham Playhouse in 1970, and though it subsequently came to London for some weeks at the Old Vic, the National Theatre's temporary home, this was still the period of eclipse for Fry's plays, and it did not have a long London run. The play is subtitled "A Summer Comedy," and the summer is an Italian summer, based on Fry's memories of living in Italy—hot to the point of discomfort, waterless (in this case), ominous with storms, like the one that flooded the sewers and is still lurking: "There's a snake of lightning twitching low on the hills / Towards Arezzo" (96). The heat is oppressive as well as beneficent, but the play is still a comedy in theme and texture. As in the earlier comedies, the imagery usually is funny as well as amplifying the dialogue, and the characters occasionally use other kinds of linguistic humor, such as Roberto's scrambled proverb— "Don't cross your bridge till you see it collapsing" (5)—and Luigi's mixed metaphors—"If we . . . build up heavy industry, / Pump money into the dry cisterns, / Prosperity snowballs" (77). Comic reversals abound. From being the unmentionable black sheep, Edmondo becomes his father's pride and joy; his lavishly bestowed gifts are unwanted; Luigi "wins" the race; and all these surprises are turned to a good end. Cesare's message is to "insist on all the powers that recover us" (104), a deeper prospect of hope for humanity in general, while the individual characters are happy with, or at least reconciled to, their various lots, a reconciliation symbolized in the oldest tradition of comedy with the final wedding prospect of Roberto and Grazia.

Chapter Eleven

A Song or Half-song:
One Thing More

Chelmsford Cathedral and the BBC jointly commissioned a play from Fry in 1986. Although Fry recollects having written a poem as a schoolboy about Caedmon, he cast around for some time before thinking of this subject, an inspiration that coincidentally occurred to his radio producer, Jane Morgan, simultaneously. Caedmon is one of the blessed poets of religious history and thus a suitable subject for a religious festival play. He is an unlettered peasant, and his story is a simple one, as told by Bede in his *Ecclesiastical History*. Fry widened the significance of this little tale by giving Caedmon a motive beyond natural inarticulacy for the silence and suffering of the first part of his life, before the poetry begins for him.

As the play opens, Caedmon, a stranger, is being discussed with suspicion by the natives of the Whitby area; he speaks to no one, is staying in a cave, and haunts the outskirts of the abbey with strange persistence. First an inquisitive widow and then the farm overman question him and elicit from him that his name is Caedmon, a Celtic name, that he has been a mercenary soldier, that he was born at Rookhope, and, unclearly, that he has come to the monastery to gain information about someone who may be living there. One of the epigraphs to the play is taken from Sophocles' *Philoctetes*, and the scene-setting discussion, followed by a prolonged question-and-answer sequence, is the same in both plays, though Caedmon is evasive and inarticulate, as well as terse, in his replies. This part of the play closes with the generous offer by the still-baffled overman of work in the farm stables.

A scene at the monastery follows in which a novice nun is seeking help from Abbess Hilda for the distractions of memory or curiosity that are intruding on her worship of God. She is becoming obsessed with thoughts of her unknown parents—her mother dead, her father fled—and never mentioned by the grandparents who had brought her up. Possibly the audience will have guessed even before she mentions Rookhope as her birthplace that the novice is Caedmon's daughter, the person whose dwelling place he was anxious to see. This is not, however, a play about sentimental family reunio

The abbess's advice to the novice is that she should relate her anxieties to God, regarding them not as sin but as part of her complex offering to God's service, and this thematically prefigures what Caedmon also has to learn about his own problems.

The play next shows Caedmon, tongue-tied but regarded with liking, working with the other villagers. A solar eclipse has shaken the community, and during an evening of festivity to celebrate and confirm the return of natural daylight, all the villagers take turn singing. Caedmon slips out before his turn, and in spite of the friendly protests and encouragement of those who try to stop him, he goes to his stable loft to sleep. This is the midpoint of the short play; in spite of his acceptance by the village community, Caedmon is still essentially at odds with the rest of the world, separated from other human beings: "He was sick with himself for never finding, even for the sake of mirth, words that would make a bridge between himself and his fellow men," explains Bede as narrator.[1]

At this low point when Caedmon feels himself forever apart, he dreams that he is in his seacliff cave again, experiencing a vision that is much expanded from Bede's brief description and in the form of an argument with a dream figure, who refers to it as a wrestling, like the wrestling of Jacob and the angel. The dream figure draws from Caedmon the buried causes of his separation from life. Caedmon feels both an outcast and a rebel. Thirty years previously his happiness had been shattered when the girl he loved died in childbirth at the age of sixteen—"I gave death to her" (28)—and the suffering and injustice of this loss has locked him into a lifelong silent resentment against God. Like the younger Cesare in *A Yard of Sun,* he hates himself and the universe where such injustice is permitted; to confirm this, he has become a mercenary soldier to confront what he sees as the destructiveness of God in its more open manifestations. In the course of the debate, a vision of the dead girl tells him not to let her be lost in silence and that he must trust and accept a hidden purpose if he wishes to be reunited with her. This is a turning point of the argument and of Caedmon's life; he now sees the girl as still existing and as communicating with him if he trusts God's will. As he accepts, the power to sing inspires him; he responds to the figure's commands and sings of the creation of the world.

The song is still with him when he wakes and in time is noticed by the overman, who, amazed at his sudden powers, insists on taking Caedmon to the abbess. The first interview with abbess, prior, and precentor, during which they hear Caedmon's song and set him a test of composing another song on a specified subject, is compressed into a few lines of narrative by Bede, and only the second interview is dramatized at length. The prior still wonders whether "what he recited to us hadn't been prepared over a length of time, and given this dream story to impress us" (35), but Caedmon, after some modest demurral that causes suspense, duly produces a song on the subject of the Israelites' escape from Egypt through the wilderness. All are convinced of the genuineness of his inspiration, and after he has left the precentor remembers having seen him previously on a battlefield, in circumstances Caedmon hinted at in "I gave my sword to a flooded river" (15), at the turning point when he gave up fighting and helped the monks to tend the wounded.

The acknowledgment of Caedmon's inspiration, its validation by the saintly abbess, is the second climax of Caedmon's story, and after this, Bede briefly narrates the remainder of Caedmon's life almost to its end: how he is persuaded to join the monastery and become part of its music. No recognition of the novice nun ever takes place; he has accepted the past and is at peace. One final scene shows his deathbed. He speaks of his life: "These not-so-many years, what vastness has filled them, though I made so little of it" (42). He knows he is dying but would "like to make one thing more, a song or half-song or no song, but one thing more in thanksgiving for having seen and known and lived and died" (42). So he speaks one last song, comparing his death to a childhood reluctance to leave the day's play with its dust and sunlight. He is now ready to stop loitering like a reluctant child and leave earthly time: "Listen," he says. "Where I break off, the music is filling my place" (43).

The text of the play is preceded by three "forenotes," consisting of quotations from Bede's *Ecclesiastical History*, Sophocles' *Philoctetes*, and Genesis 32:24–29. The first briefly tells of Caedmon's dream, his transformation from one who "cannot sing" to one who can; the second describes the cave and belongings of the absent Philoctetes, the man who was marooned by his fellow Greeks on the way to Troy because of his crippling and offensive wound; and the Genesis story tells of Jacob's wrestling with the angel, who puts Jacob's thigh out of joint but blesses him before leaving. These three—Caedmon, Philoctetes, and Jacob—are flawed and suffer but are destined to find reconciliation and healing. Caedmon not only suffers from inarticulacy and a speech impediment but limps because of a battle wound to his leg, which links him with Philoctetes and Jacob. These flaws symbolize the problem of pain and evil, a problem that cuts off those who wrestle with it from the rest of the world, as well as from God. Thomas Mendip is expressing a similar rejection of life in his demand to be hanged, and it appears again when Henry Curtmantle curses God.

Caedmon's bleakness also comes from his own experience. He blames first

himself for the girl's death—"I gave death to her . . . I was the destroyer"
—and then goes on to blame God: "Why should God make woman for a
man's worship, to covet her beauty and make it his own, for death and guilt
to come of it? Where's the mercy in that?" (29). In becoming a mercenary soldier, he has willfully confronted the problem of pain and evil in its most evident forms: "I had seen God in life and He had given me death . . . I saw him
only in the pain, in the unloving sword-hacking violence—and hoped his
eyes were covered, in a shame for his own making" (29). Somehow—and this
has to be understood as the effect of the vision of the girl as still continuing to
exist elsewhere—Caedmon is convinced that he must accept God's will, including the suffering and evil, and by accepting he is reunited with God. Silence has been his protest against evil, and when, during his impassioned
condemnation of God's destruction, the person in the dream laughingly says,
"Where is your silence now?" Caedmon retorts fiercely, "What I'm saying *is*
the silence" (29).

The songs are the more impressive as they contrast with Caedmon's otherwise laconic, hesitant prose. His simple list of what he absorbs from the
atmosphere—"the colour of the stone, the sound of the sea, the lowing and
the bleating and the cock-crow and the voice of the bell" (15)—is amplified
by Bede: "His head was full of the sounds of life, calling from over the hill,
wind blowing and the flowing water, the alarm cry and skyward singing of
birds, the lowing and whinneying and bleating and cackling of living crea-
tures with their utterances, the cries, prayers and laughter of men and
women." It is then shaped into Caedmon's first song about the creation of the
Earth:

> And called it Earth, in water-and-air-life eager,
> Under tides, or wings clouding the brightness,
> And creatures warm in their eyes, the day possessing,
> The secret night invading.
>
> (34)

The first song looks outward at the created world—ironically Bede's original
History claims that Caedmon's songs made many "despise the world"—
while the second looks inward.[2] The Israelites' wandering becomes an image
for the course of individual experience, the "soon-over of life," which is nonetheless a "great journey, / Hard and far to the flesh of the foot, / Hard to the
scarred mind" (38). The song asks, "Have you brought me to say that every
true journey / Starts in a storm of pain?" as has been Caedmon's own experience, and his pain identifies him with the Egyptian victims of "the throb,

throb of death-wings passing over" (38), but at last he has come to see himself as one of the Israelites, going on to the reconciliation of innocence after guilt, "not Eden, but Eden forgiven, / Or at least echoed in water under the palm-trees" (38).

The movement of this second song is more complex than the hymn of praise for the Creation: hope conflicts with weakness and faintheartedness:

> In the setting-out hopes were high,
> Larksong no higher, trumpets of liberation
> Drowned all the lamentation of Egypt.
> And God was vanguard and rearguard
> And a way through the deep waters.
> Hearts failed them still, bodies broke,
> There was anger, terror, despair still, there was death:
> But always a pillar of cloud by day
> Paced that shadow of people moving across the wilderness.
>
> (38)

Although Caedmon is a Briton, as the widow notices, the historical poem of Caedmon is in Anglo-Saxon language and traditional form, and here Fry's version has also an element of alliteration, but it is recurrent without being insistent; for instance, in the passage just quoted, the repetition of *h, l, w, b, d* needs searching out. One critic of the second production in Chelsea Old Church compared the style to that of Hopkins, an impression probably created by the alliterative effect, the suppression of articles, and the linked nouns: "by God-love given," "in water-and-air-life," "flower and fruit of the rib-stem" (31, 32), though again this imitates Anglo-Saxon word formation.[3]

The plot is designed to bring out Fry's recurrent theme of the hidden pattern toward which life is forever aspiring and which is individually achieved through pain and enlightenment by Caedmon. The imagery illustrating this theme pervades the whole play, not just the songs. The dominant images are again drawn from water, especially the sea, and music. Caedmon has thrown his sword into a river, which washes away the warlike part of his life, and the person in the dream tells him that experience is itself like a rough but effective river: "The water that turns the perfect wheel is turbulent" (29). Water in the desert naturally suggests relief and pleasure, so within the allegory of the Israelites' pilgrimage across the wilderness, their earthly reward is seen in terms of a "place where water comes laughing from the rock" and the ultimate union with God as "distance upon a distance to the utmost sea" (39). In Bede's de-

scription of Caedmon's dream, however, the sea becomes the life force working within and through him to bear him onward to a higher stage of spiritual
development: "The sea intoned its regular responses, sighed back into itself
to let the next wave of intercession roll towards the shuddering 'And let our
cry come unto Thee.' In Caedmon's unconscious consciousness he was borne
on the wave, or was he himself the water of the wave drawn towards the waiting land?" (26).

Music, as reflecting God's pattern of things, is the central image for the
man who had been "part of the music then" in his own lost Eden of youth and
happiness, "like the sound of evening in a garden. A burning sword drove me
out" (28). For thirty years "there was no music in himself, he knew that" (26),
but when the person releases him from silence, he finds music as an expression of God's will, "the indwelling music that created us" (31), here repeating the exact words Ana-Clara used in *A Yard of Sun* to express the same
concept. Caedmon as a monk becomes "himself a part of the music" (41), the
music replacing him as he dies.

One Thing More is written mainly in prose because, Fry says, he wanted to
establish a difference between the ordinary dialogue and the heavenly inspired songs. Caedmon's prose draws considerable force from its terseness
and the fuller meaning compressed into the few lines he manages to utter, at
least until the person in the dream goads him to justify his silence, and his
sentences become longer. The other farmworkers are more loquacious and
colorful in their speech. In an article, Fry argues that poetry is latent or potential in the speech of all individuals, and he cites dialogue reported between
two poachers after an accidental shooting, which began, "I looked at Arthur
and saw that he stood withering on his feet," and here, Fry says, poetry and
common speech have become one ("Poetry and the Theatre," 9). This example is not unlike the phrases the farmworkers use to try to express the effect of
the eclipse: "you suddenly feel life draining out of the air around you," says
one, and another asks, "When that creeping night-in-day took us over, did
your knees begin to sag?" (20). These characters are, like the supporting roles
in *The Boy with a Cart*, only sketched in—the overman is kindly, the widow
inquisitive and easily offended—but not developed; their general friendliness helps in winning Caedmon toward a wish, at least, to be united with this
human community, before the dream shows him the way.

Caedmon and Abbess Hilda, the dominant characters, are a further embodiment of the soldier and the lady who reappear in most of Fry's plays.
Compared with the earlier soldiers and ex-soldiers, such as Moses, Thomas
Mendip, and Roberto Bruno, Caedmon is humble and retiring; his evasion of
the villagers is caused not only by his speech defect but a conviction that his

life, past and future, is not of any importance. Even after the miraculous inspiration of song and the curing of his wound, he rejects the overman's ambi-
tious images for his experience and reverts to his own brief sentences: "I can't
tell you everything. Or take it all in myself" (34). Modestly he offers his test
poem to the abbess: "some sort of speaking found its way through my thick
skull in the end" (37). Because of his modest expectation, he is content to
contribute what he can, although "the real sound is always at a great remove,
unobtainable, at least by me" (37). Unlike Richard Gettner, failed writer and
failed soldier, who was driven to despair by the great remove between inspiration and achievement, Caedmon is grateful to produce even a shadow of
what he has perceived.

The Abbess Hilda has a smaller part to play but is clearly an enlightened,
intelligent, witty woman cast in the same mold as the Countess Rosmarin in
Dark. Skeptical about the "great and godly men" who have been debating
the correct way to calculate when to celebrate Easter, she shows a similar cautious skepticism about the supernatural forces that the novice nun fears: "Let
us, with very proper respect, leave the devil aside for the present. Curiosity is
not the devil; unanswered questions are not the devil" (18). Positively, she is
aware of God's pattern of things and tries to reassert the Christian values for
the combative churchmen at the synod: "I had to remind them that patience,
justice, humility and all charitableness were warmth enough to light this
house" (17). At the same time, she has time to advise the novice nun to bring
all the different, conflicting qualities of her humanity to God. When
Caedmon is brought to her, she is the most ready to believe in his divine
inspiration.

This most recent play by Fry echoes several of his earlier works: the refer-
ence to the escape of the Israelites from *The Firstborn*, the Briton bringing
God's word from *Thor*, the rejection of the world or of God, as expressed by
Thomas Mendip or Henry Curtmantle, the eclipse from *Venus*, the powerful,
saintly chatelaine figure from *Dark*, and Ana-Clara's words from *Yard*: "the
indwelling music that created us." These lesser echoes underline the fact that
Fry's ideas and themes have been consistent throughout his eleven plays. *One
Thing More* unites the ideas of the evolutionary development of humanity,
individually and together, beyond the temporary and temporal sufferings of
each one, and the rejoicing no less in the beauties of the world of "earthly
time" although accepting that they must be relinquished in due course. The
balance of this and other worldliness is at the center of all of Fry's plays, secular and religious.

Conclusion

He was saying—or so it seems to me—that there is an angle of experience
where the dark is distilled into light: either here or hereafter, in or out of
time: where our tragic fate finds itself with perfect pitch, and goes straight
to the key which creation was composed in. And comedy senses and
reaches out to this experience. It says, in effect, that groaning as we may be,
we move in the figure of a dance, and, so moving, we trace the outline of
the mystery.[1]

Fry was paraphrasing his friend the writer Charles Williams and at the
same time giving an account his own overall comic vision. Not all of Fry's
plays are comedies, but his vision gives the angle of experience in which
tragedies can be seen as part of a larger productive pattern. Ultimately all
that seems evil and intolerable in experience will be recompensed, or seen as
necessary, or healed. Even the tragic waste of lives such as Shendi's in *The
Firstborn*, Hoel's in *Thor*, and the girl's in *One Thing More*, will receive a
blessing, "out of time."

For the individual like Cuthman or Caedmon, a sense of personal salvation and faith in God is sufficient, but in most of the plays, the figure of a
dance is the larger scale pattern of spiritual evolution for all the human
race. Fry arrived at this idea independently but comments that he had been
pleased later to find it formulated more fully in the writings of Teilhard de
Chardin. The effort of one saint is not enough; as Teilhard de Chardin says,
humanity as a whole has "the lineaments of one single and gigantic organ-
ism" and "only progresses by slowly elaborating."[2] Piecemeal, human beings have to strive for their own spiritual insight and their sense of being
part of the onward evolutionary movement. At the same time, this movement is being assisted by pressure from God, perhaps felt as the force of
life, and because this is the same pressure that keeps plants and animals, the
rose, the thistle, in their more static places in the pattern, acceptance of the
evolutionary force is often seen in terms of natural imagery, although this
has to be distinguished from the temptation to be merely natural—to vege-
tate retrogressively.

The problem in staging Fry's plays is to achieve the right balance between
the playwright's assurance that "good is itself" (3:54) and must be pursued,
and the evils that appear in the plays—the deaths in *Firstborn*, the torture in

Lady, Cesare's imprisonment in the concentration camp. Although Fry first saw his comedies in terms of tragedy, he considered with some concern that the comic writing then tended to overwhelm the tragic element; his intention that, for instance, *Venus* should show "life being lived in the knowledge of death" had not been realized "in the production, or in the writing either."[3] Similarly he had meant *Lady* to be "something tougher and darker. . . . I aimed at a balance between darkness and light."[4] Contrary to Kenneth Tynan's opinion, then, Fry's plays do need "sombre pointing and emphases" to gain this balance between dark and light.[5] Moreover, Fry's ideas of spiritual evolution are not explained fully in the comedies, and if this dimension of "the mystery" is to be absorbed even partly by audiences, seriousness must not be sacrificed to a comic ideal of more laughs per line.

The other possible problem in staging Fry's plays—the fact that they are unusual in their verse form—has never been a problem. Like Eliot, Fry was aware of the lack of a living tradition of poetic drama: "No generally accepted belief or attitude exists today as a place to start from; no generally accepted form of play either—as the Greeks had, and the Elizabethans had, and the Restoration dramatists had, which by its expectedness prepared the ground for communication. Nor is there any style of writing which playwrights hold in common, as a base from which to start on their personal explorations, and a place from which the audience can make its judgement. Do we have to evolve a kind of esperanto of the theatre to speak to the many-headed monster of the auditorium?" ("Looking for a Language," 7). However, expectations about form and language of plays were more of a disadvantage than otherwise to Fry. Earlier misgivings about the acceptability of verse drama, and subsequent assumptions that it had been definitely extinguished, shown up as a literary dead end, by the resurgence of realism in the theater, were unfounded as far as audiences were concerned and are even less valid in the current eclectic theatrical climate. As with the vague, normative critical idea that all plays would approximate as nearly as possible to the well-made play blueprint, critics did seem to expect that verse drama would have a strong rhythm, if not rhyme, and Fry's language was attacked as not being poetry at all because its meter was not strong enough; rather, it was prose chopped up into short lines. This nostalgia for blank verse did not affect audiences at the first productions and is not likely to occur to audiences today.

Fry's plays have passed through the common cycle of great popularity followed by neglect but are now accepted as valid products of their time. The unfashionably aristocratic settings of *Venus* and *Dark,* which made these plays antipathetic to some contemporary theatergoers of the fifties and sixties, have become an accepted factor of their period of writing. Like many other playwrights of the twentieth century, Fry, though not yet revived in the West End, continues to be performed on television, on radio, all over England in provincial theaters, and all over the world.

Notes and References

Preface

1. *An Experience of Critics* (London: Perpetua, 1952), 23 (hereafter cited parenthetically in the text).
2. See the description of this effect in Katharine Worth, "Eliot and the Living Theatre," in *Eliot in Perspective,* ed. Graham Martin (London: Macmillan, 1970), 154.
3. "Talking of Henry," *Twentieth Century* 169 (February 1961):189 (hereafter cited parenthetically in the text).

Chapter One

1. Arnold Hinchcliffe, *Modern Verse Drama* (London: Methuen, 1977), 55.
2. *Can You Find Me* (Oxford: Oxford University Press, 1978), 17 (hereafter cited parenthetically in the text).
3. Christopher Fry, *Plays* (London: Oxford University Press, 1969–1971), 1, 3 (hereafter cited parenthetically in the text).
4. Robert Gittings, "The Smell of Sulphur," *Encounter* 50, no. 1 (January 1978):73.

Chapter Two

1. T. S. Eliot, *Selected Prose,* ed. John Hayward (London: Penguin, 1953), 42.
2. Ibid., 57.
3. Ibid., 76.
4. Ibid., 77.
5. Ibid., 76.
6. Ibid., 79.
7. Ibid.
8. Ibid., 16.
9. T. S. Eliot, Introduction to S. L. Bethell, *Shakespeare and the Popular Dramatic Tradition* (London: Staple Press, 1944).
10. "Poetry and the Theatre," *Adam* 19 (1951):9 (hereafter cited parenthetically in the text).
11. T. S. Eliot, *Complete Poems and Plays* (London: Faber, 1969), 240.
12. Ibid.
13. Ibid.
14. Ibid., 244.

15. Ibid., 282.

Chapter Three

1. Exodus 7:13.
2. Denis Donoghue, *The Third Voice* (Princeton and London: Princeton University Press, 1959), 182.
3. Kenneth Pickering, *Drama in the Cathedral* (London: Churchman, 1986), 298.

Chapter Four

1. Jeremy Taylor, *The Golden Grove: Selected Passages from the Sermons and Writings of Jeremy Taylor*, ed. Logan Pearsall Smith (Oxford: Oxford University Press, 1930), 157.
2. Ibid., 158.
3. Ibid., 157.
4. Stanley M. Wiersma, *More Than the Ear Discovers* (Chicago: Loyola University Press, 1983), 75.
5. Ibid., 87.
6. *Death Is a Kind of Love* (London: Tidal Press, 1979).
7. "FDJ," *Theatre World* (June 1946):7.

Chapter Five

1. *Daily Telegraph,* 11 March 1948, 2.
2. *Times,* 11 March 1948, 2.
3. *New Statesman and Nation*, 20 March 1948, 233.
4. *Times,* 12 May 1949, 7.
5. W. Heinrich von Riehl, "Wooing the Gallows," in *The Masterpiece Library of Short Stories, vol. 7: Old German*, ed. J. A. Hammerton (London: The Educational Book Co., n.d.) 299–307.
6. *New Statesman and Nation*, 20 March 1948, 233.
7. *Times,* 12 May 1949, 7.
8. *New Statesman and Nation*, 21 May 1949, 527.
9. *Theatre World* (June 1949):11–12.
10. *Observer,* 14 March 1948, 2.

Chapter Six

1. "Venus Considered," *Theatre Newsletter*, 11 March 1950, 5 (hereafter cited parenthetically in the text).
2. Nicholas Berdyaev, *Freedom and the Spirit*, trans. Oliver Fielding (London: Bles, 1935), 203.
3. Ibid., 205.

4. *Chichester Festival Theatre Programme*, August 1988.

5. Peter Brook, "Venus Observed," *Adam* 19 (1951):18.

6. *Punch*, 5 January 1950, 105.

7. *New Statesman and Nation*, 28 January 1950, 96–97.

8. *Sunday Dispatch*, 22 January 1950, 6.

9. *Sunday Times*, 22 January 1950, 5.

10. Ibid., 19 January 1950, 2.

11. Ibid.

12. William B. Wahl, "A Visit to the Toft: Interview with Christopher Fry," in *Salzburg Studies in English* (Salzburg: University of Salzburg, 1977), 562.

13. His views reported privately to Fry after the production.

Chapter Seven

1. *Plays and Players* (May 1954):13.

2. Fry points to her readiness to be persuaded by Janik (3:93) as a willingness to be convinced even of the necessity of military action, if good enough reasons can be produced.

3. Wiersma, *More Than the Ear Discovers*, 183.

4. Ibid., 182.

5. *Observer*, 2 May 1954, 11.

6. *Sunday Times*, 2 May 1954, 11.

7. *Punch*, 12 May 1954, 29.

Chapter Eight

1. *Theatre World* (July 1951):10.

2. Wiersma, *More Than the Ear Discovers*, 298.

3. *Sunday Times*, 27 May 1951, 2.

4. *New Statesman and Nation*, 26 May 1951, 591.

5. *Sunday Times*, 27 May 1951, 2.

6. *Observer*, 20 May 1951, 6.

Chapter Nine

1. "Looking for a Language," *Adam* (1980):10.

2. "Theatre and History," *Essays and Studies* 30 (1977):86 (hereafter cited parenthetically in the text).

3. *Spectator*, 19 October 1962, 596–97.

4. Ibid., 597.

5. *Illustrated London News*, 20 October 1962, 622.

6. *Sunday Times*, 14 October 1962, 41.

7. *Spectator*, 19 October 1962, 596.

Chapter Ten

1. *Masterpiece Library of Short Stories*, vol. 17.
2. *A Yard of Sun* (London: Oxford University Press, 1970), 102 (hereafter cited parenthetically in the text).
3. This echoes a description of a visionary state in Revelation 21:23–25: "the city had no need of the sun or moon to shine upon it, for the glory of God gave it light."

Chapter Eleven

1. *One Thing More* (London: King's College London, 1986), 26 (hereafter cited parenthetically in the text).
2. Bede, *Bede's Ecclesiastical History of the English People*, ed. Bertram Colgrave and R. A. B. Mynors (Oxford: Oxford University Press, 1969), 415.
3. Harry Eyres, *Times*, 4 November 1988, 5.

Conclusion

1. "Comedy," *Tulane Drama Review* 4, no. 3 (1960):77.
2. P. Teilhard de Chardin, *The Phenomenon of Man* (London: Wm. Collins, Sons & Co., 1959), 112, 180.
3. Wahl, "A Visit at the Toft: Interview with Christopher Fry," 562.
4. Ibid., 561.
5. Kenneth Tynan, *He That Plays the King* (London: Longmans Green, 1950), 144.

Selected Bibliography

PRIMARY WORKS

Collected Works

Plays, London: Oxford University Press, 1969. Contains *A Phoenix Too Frequent, Thor, with Angels,* and *The Lady's Not for Burning.*

Plays, London: Oxford University Press, 1970. Contains *The Boy with a Cart, The Firstborn,* and *Venus Observed.*

Plays, London: Oxford University Press, 1971. Contains *A Sleep of Prisoners, The Dark Is Light Enough,* and *Curtmantle.*

Giraudoux: Three Plays (translated), Oxford: Oxford University Press, 1963. Contains *Tiger at the Gates, Duel of Angels,* and *Judith.*

Individual Plays

The Boy with a Cart. London: Oxford University Press, 1939.

The Firstborn. Cambridge: Cambridge University Press, 1946. 2d rev. ed. London: Oxford University Press, 1952.

A Phoenix Too Frequent. London: Hollis and Carter Ltd., 1946.

Thor, with Angels. First published in an acting edition, Canterbury: H. J. Goulden, 1948. 2d ed., London: Oxford University Press, 1949.

The Lady's Not for Burning. London: Oxford University Press, 1949. Rev. ed., London: Oxford University Press, 1950.

Venus Observed. London: Oxford University Press, 1950.

A Sleep of Prisoners. London: Oxford University Press, 1951.

The Dark Is Light Enough. London: Oxford University Press, 1954.

Curtmantle. London: Oxford University Press, 1965. Rev. ed., London: Oxford University Press, 1965.

A Yard of Sun. London: Oxford University Press, 1970.

The Brontës of Haworth. 2 vols. London: Davis-Poynter, 1975 (television playscript).

One Thing More. London: King's College London, 1986. New York, 1987.

Translations

Anouilh, Jean. *Ring around the Moon: A Charade with Music (L'Invitation au château).* London: Methuen, 1951.

————. *The Lark (L'Alouette).* London: Methuen, 1956.

Giraudoux, Jean. *Tiger at the Gates (La Guerre de Troie n'aura pas lieu).* London: Methuen, 1955.
_____. *Duel of Angels (Pour Lucrèce).* London: Oxford University Press, 1959.
_____. *Judith.* London: Oxford University Press, 1961.
Ibsen, Henrik. *Peer Gynt.* London: Oxford University Press, 1970.
Rostand, Edmond. *Cyrano de Bergerac.* London: Oxford University Press, 1975.

Other Writings

"Comedy." *Adelphi* (November 1950):27–29.
"Poetry and the Theatre." *Adam* 19 (1951):2–10.
An Experience of Critics. London: Perpetua, 1952.
"How Lost, How Amazed, How Miraculous We Are." *Theatre Arts* 36 (August 1952):27.
"Why Verse?" *World Theatre* 4, no. 4 (1955):51–61.
"Comedy." *Tulane Drama Review* 4, no. 3 (1960):77–79.
The Boat That Mooed. New York: Macmillan, 1965.
"Talking of Henry." *Twentieth Century* 169 (February 1961):186–90.
"Theatre and History." *Essays and Studies* 30 (1977):86–87.
Can You Find Me. London: Oxford University Press, 1978.
Death Is a Kind of Love. London: 1979.
"Looking for a Language." *Adam* (1980):428–30.
Genius, Talent and Failure: The Brontës. Adam Lecture, 1986. London: King's College London, 1987.

SECONDARY WORKS

Books

Browne, E. Martin. *Two in One.* Cambridge: Cambridge University Press, 1981. An autobiography, with some details of early Fry productions.
Donoghue, Denis. *The Third Voice: Modern British and American Verse Drama.* Princeton and London: Princeton University Press, 1959. Comments on Fry's style from a hostile point of view.
Evans, Gareth Lloyd. *The Language of Modern Drama.* London: Dent, 1977. Mainly on the context and development of the poetic drama movement, with a little mention of Fry.
Hinchcliffe, Arnold. *Modern Verse Drama.* London: Methuen, 1977. Discusses Fry's development and contemporary significance.
Leeming, Glenda. *Poetic Drama.* London: Macmillan, 1989. Contains a chapter on Fry's language and ideas.

Merchant, W. Moelwyn. *Creed and Drama: An Essay in Religious Drama.* Philadelphia: Fortress, 1965. A sympathetic discussion of Fry's religious ideas.

Pickering, Kenneth. *Drama in the Cathedral: The Canterbury Festival Plays 1928–48.* London: Churchman, 1958. Discusses background of plays performed at Canterbury Festival, including a critical account of *Thor, with Angels.*

Roy, Emil. *Christopher Fry.* Carbondale and Edwardsville: Southern Illinois University Press, 1968. A straightforward discussion of Fry's plays up to and including *Curtmantle.*

Spanos, William V. *The Christian Tradition in Modern British Verse Drama.* New Brunswick, N.J.: Rutgers University Press, 1967. Includes a section on Fry, discussing mainly his ideas.

Stanford, Derek. *Christopher Fry: An Appreciation.* London: Peter Nevill, 1951. Full and heavily philosophical exposition of plays and their plots.

————. *Christopher Fry.* Writers and Their Works Series. London: Longmans, 1954; rev. 1962. A shorter account of Fry's plays than the previously cited book.

————. *A Christopher Fry Album.* London: Peter Nevill, 1952. Detailed and anecdotal though not always accurate biography of Fry with descriptions of early productions; several nice photographs.

Weales, Gerald. *Religion in Modern English Drama.* Philadelphia: University of Pennsylvania Press, 1961. Extensive description of religious drama movement since around 1900, with occasional dismissive mention of Fry.

Wiersma, Stanley M. *Christopher Fry.* Contemporary Writers in Christian Perspective Series. Michigan: Wm. B. Eerdmans, 1969. Contains some interesting comments not included in the longer work cited next.

————. *More Than the Ear Discovers: God in the Plays of Christopher Fry.* Chicago: Loyola University Press, 1983. The fullest and most helpful study so far, concentrating on the ideas of the plays rather than performance.

Vos, Nelvin. *The Drama of Comedy, Victim and Victor.* Richmond, Va.: Knox, 1966. Includes a section on Fry, applying a theory of the religious nature of all comedy, incorporating sacrificial suffering and redemption.

Articles and Parts of Books

Anderson, B. W. "The Poetry of Mr. Fry." *Spectator,* 31 March 1950, 432. Appreciative account of Fry's style.

Bewley, Marius. "The Verse of Christopher Fry." *Scrutiny* 18 (June 1951):78–84. A critical condemnation of Fry's style from the *Scrutiny* point of view.

Browne, E. Martin. *Verse in the Modern English Theatre.* W. D. Thomas Memorial Lecture. Cardiff, 1963. Valedictory account of verse drama movement; interesting on Fry's *The Firstborn.*

————. "Poetry in the English Theatre." *Proceedings of the Royal Institute of Great*

Britain 34 (1952):287–93. History of religious drama movement, with little mention of Fry.

Ferguson, John. "The Boy with a Cart." *Modern Drama* 8 (1965):284–92. Discusses unpretentious yet numinous religious effect of play.

_____. "Christopher Fry's *A Sleep of Prisoners.*" *English* 10 (1954):42–47. Discusses interwoven themes of play.

Findlater, Richard. "The Two Countesses." *Twentieth Century* 156 (August 1954):175. Criticizes static nature of play in first production.

Gillespie, Diane Filby. "Language and Life: Christopher Fry's Early Plays." *Modern Drama* 21 (1978):287–96. Argues for Fry's reconciliation of theme of decay with linguistic life.

Gittings, Robert. "The Smell of Sulphur." *Encounter* 50 (January 1978): 73–78. Biographical comments on *The Lady's Not for Burning.*

Greene, Ann. "Fry's Cosmic Vision." In *Experimental Drama.* Edited by W. A. Armstrong. London: Bell, 1963. Emphasizes philosophical point of view of plays.

Kerr, Walter. "Christopher Fry." In *Essays in Modern Drama.* Edited by Morris Freedman. Boston: Heath, 1966. Discusses Fry's work up to *Curtmantle.*

Lecky, Eleazer. "Mystery in the Plays of Christopher Fry." *Tulane Drama Review* 4 (1960):80–87. Diagnoses different kinds of mystery, in the religious sense, in Fry's plays.

Muir, Kenneth. "Verse and Prose." In *Contemporary Theatre*, 96–115. Edited by J. R. Brown and Bernard Harris. Stratford-on-Avon Studies 4. London: Edward Arnold, 1962. General survey of poetic drama from Yeats to Eliot.

Spender, Stephen. "Christopher Fry." *Spectator* 184 (1950):364. Discusses Fry's language.

Wahl, William B. "A Visit at the Toft: Interview with Christopher Fry." In *Salzburg Studies in English Literature*, 546–72. Directed by P. Erwin Sturtzl. Salzburg: University of Salzburg, 1977. Useful in eliciting Fry's views on his own practice.

Woodfield, James. "'The Figure of a Dance': Christopher Fry's *A Phoenix Too Frequent.*" *Ariel* 9 (July 1978):3–19. Finds a common death and resurrection motif in all Fry's plays.

Index